Horsemanship and Life

A True Story

Also by Michelle R. Scully:

Broken, Tales of a Titanium Cowgirl

Horsemanship and Life

A True Story

Michelle R. Scully

Copyright © 2022 by Michelle R. Scully

ALL RIGHTS RESERVED. No part of this book may be reproduced or transmitted in any form by any means, electronic or mechanical, including photocopying and recording, or by any information storage and retrieval system, except as may be expressly permitted in writing from the publisher. Requests for permission should be addressed to Spinning Sevens Press, Attn: Rights and Permissions, P.O. Box 440 Floyd, Virginia, 24091.

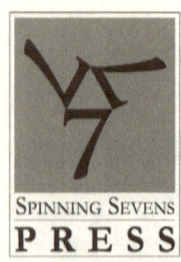

ISBN 978-0-9992465-7-3
Cover photo by Sierra Baker.
Cover designed by Emily Kitching.

Dedication

To Clementine and Simba
I'll never understand how anyone thought you were throw away
animals
When you were the ones with all the answers
and
To Scout and Kai
For refilling our hearts and helping us be better humans
each and every day
And to my little mom,
for showing me what faith in action looks like

Contents

Acknowledgments ....*i*

Introduction ....*ii*

Photo Credits ....*v*

One	A True Story...1
Two	Horsemanship and Life..5
Three	Clementine's Cat Tales..8
Four	Things Clem Taught Me, or Lessons from a Cat......11
Five	Today I'm (Still) Good..16
Six	Just a Mare..19
Seven	New Partners...23
Eight	Maisy Mae...26
Nine	The Universe is Sneaky, or Hello Calamity Jane.......30
Ten	The World According to Rufus...................................33
Eleven	Horse Hunting..36
Twelve	Hello Handsome..38
Thirteen	Animal Farm 41
Fourteen	Begin at the Beginning..45
Fifteen	Do the Work..48
Sixteen	Making a Horse From the Inside Out........................50

Seventeen	Stupid Horses	52
Eighteen	New Boy in Town	54
Nineteen	My Hindsight's 20/40	56
Twenty	A Place of Neutral	59
Twenty-One	Have a Heart	61
Twenty-Two	Inner Life	63
Twenty-Three	A Place of Peace	65
Twenty-Four	Wait for It	68
Twenty-Five	Blind Date	71
Twenty-Six	I Choose You	74
Twenty-Seven	A Better Deal	77
Twenty-Eight	Salty Ears	80
Twenty-Nine	Analysis Paralysis	85
Thirty	Fiddlin' Around (or, The Perfect Cure for Analysis Paralysis)	89
Thirty-One	See It, Feel It, Trust It	93
Thirty-Two	(If) Patience is a Virtue	96
Thirty-Three	The Spirit of It All	98
Thirty-Four	Honoring the Wisdom of Years	100
Thirty-Five	Inside Out	103
Thirty-Six	Is the Horse Water Still On?	107

Thirty-Seven	Bit by Bit	108
Thirty-Eight	Lessons from a Waitress	111
Thirty-Nine	What's the Definition of Insanity?	114
Forty	What Happened, Before What Happened Happened	117
Forty-One	Hooked on a Feeling	120
Forty-Two	The Strong Silent Type	123
Forty-Three	May I have your Attention Please, Please!	126
Forty-Four	The Wave	129
Forty-Five	Connection or Control?	132
Forty-Six	Creatures of Habit	135
Forty-Seven	Training Tools	137
Forty-Eight	Be Quiet	139
Forty-Nine	Get in the @#$% Trailer Already	141
Fifty	Imagining Dragons	144
Fifty-One	The Law of the Hammer	147
Fifty-Two	Why?	148
Fifty-Three	The Stories We Tell	153
Fifty-Four	The Fine Art of Saying Yes	155
Fifty-Five	What if?	158
Fifty-Six	Magic Eight	160

Fifty-Seven	I've Got You	164
Fifty-Eight	Soft Heart in a Hard World	166
Fifty-Nine	Last Horse, a Poem	168
Sixty	Lucky Charms	174
Sixty-One	Dreams	176
Sixty-Two	Let Go	179
Sixty-Three	When Things get Western	181
Sixty-Four	Little Things	184
Sixty-Five	Truth Serum	185
Sixty-Six	I Water This Tree	188
Sixty-Seven	Horses and Zebras	191
Sixty-Eight	Bilateral Blues	195
Sixty-Nine	Déjà vu	198
Seventy	What a Long Strange Trip It's Been	202
Seventy-One	The Tortoise and the Hare	205
Seventy-Two	Grace	209
Seventy-Three	Thank You	211
Appendix	Horsemanship and Life: Asking from a Friend	215
About the Author		223

Acknowledgements

This book is my love letter to horses
and to those of us who love them so.
Yea, we're obsessed, and a little bit weird,
but we're also a wild and wonderful and full of try bunch.
My favorite kind of people.

Thank you, Pat,
for understanding my passion
and for always picking up the barrels for the old guys.

Thank you, Tom Moates, for believing in me not just once, but twice.

And with gratitude to
Crissi, Josh, Mark
Molly, Shea, and Tom
who've been friends, mentors, and inspiration

Thank you for sharing
your thoughts about horsemanship and life
and for showing us
what a better way with horses looks like

Introduction

Half a lifetime ago, my nickname was Lucky Girl. Silly, right? I can't even really remember why. I must have been having the best time ever. But it's dangerous to be named Lucky, even if it's a nickname, like you're just asking for it and it makes the Universe want to say, "Hey, somebody, hold my beer." My dog Cassidy the Catahoula once "brought home" a rooster I mistakenly named Lucky.

He wasn't.

My summer as a blackjack dealer cured me of any idea of luck; it's all about the odds, and FYI, they're with the house. You can save yourself a lot of money if you just believe me now. I was super-hot one night, running players off with the cards firmly in my favor when a man came to my table and said, "Hey little lady (yes, he actually said that), you look lonely, I'll play at your table." I told him, "Well, Sir, I'd recommend you don't. I'm alone as I hit 21 with six cards, so I'd recommend you tuck those chips back into your pocket and cash out." He didn't listen and lost $1500 in five minutes; and just like that, I was alone again.

After my wreck and recovery (which I shared in my first book, Broken, Tales of a Titanium Cowgirl) people often said, "You're very lucky you weren't paralyzed." I could have been; my shock-induced decision to crawl up the hill after my fall could have easily changed that. Little did I know that a sharp broken vertebrae was impinging upon my spinal cord, though as a sciencey girl you'd expect better of me, but shock overrides whatever good sense system we have. Eleven years have passed since the day the rabbit ran out and changed the trajectory of my life, and fortunately my horsemanship (and life) journey has continued to expand and fills my soul daily with wonder and gratitude.

I don't believe in luck, but I do believe I'm blessed.

I liked my old unbroken body much better (I know I'm not

alone in that), but I feel so blessed to have seen how God worked all things for my good out of what for all appearances was one big fat mess.

I wanted to share the why of why I write anything, and to what end. What I've learned through my own "black sharpie line experience" is that beauty and blessings can come from a big wrecking ball of change.

I've lived it, I know it can happen, and God laid it upon my heart to share the lessons of hope and encouragement I've experienced the best I can.

And apparently the way I'm trying to do that is by weird ramblings and trying to be as real as possible about this sometimes messy, sometimes glorious, sometimes sprinkled with glitter, sometimes you-know-what-show we call life.

If I can crawl back, I know anyone can.

After Broken, Tales of a Titanium Cowgirl was published my husband Pat asked me what my definition of success would be. I had to think hard about that. I'm no JK Rowling with her extraordinarily successful books about some guy named Harry, but here's what I came up with. My definition of success, of what I want my horsemanship/life journey to count for, is in three things I hoped for.

That me sharing my story help one horse get a better deal. Horses too often get the lesser end of the deal with humans, and they deserve much more from us. They give us beauty, joy, and magic, and they deserve all the goodness we can bring to the relationship they allow us to have with them in return.

That it encourages one person. Life, and life with horses, is often fraught with unexpected dismounts and journeys we never thought we'd take. We all have experienced that black sharpie line moment, a life-changing turn forever separating "before" from "after." My belief is that we're here to shine a light on ahead for each other when the path looks too dark to navigate alone. I'm not overly skilled with a head lamp, and I have temporarily blinded myself a time or

two, but I am all about walking alongside each other through dark times.

And last, and maybe this one should be first, but I hoped that it would make my amazing publisher and wonderful horseman Tom Moates enough money that he doesn't regret believing in me and Broken, Tales of a Titanium Cowgirl and now, Horsemanship and Life: A True Story.

Not a high bar perhaps, but I feel like I've achieved all the success I could ever hope for when someone reaches out to me to say how much it's meant to them to know that they are not alone.

You are not. Please never forget that.

This horsemanship/life journey is sprinkled and blessed with some of the best, most amazing people you could ever hope to meet and they tend to be an incredibly supportive tribe. If you haven't found your people yet, keep looking because they are out there.

So that's my story, and why I write—who Lucky Girl became when she grew up and learned there is no such thing as luck, only lots of try and faith.

May huge amounts of sunshine pour down on you today.

May your path be scattered with love, faith, friendship, cats, dogs, and horses.

Always horses.

xoxo

Photo Credits

All photo credits are to Michelle R. Scully except for the following:

Page 23...Karen Pavone Photography
Page 89...Stephanie Roundy
Page 93...Jane Kameny Brown
Page 117...Jane Kameny Brown
Page 123...Stephanie Roundy
Page 137...Leslie Exter
Page 155...Stephanie Roundy
Page 164...Marie Danielsson
Page 166...Lisa Daniel
Page 169...Deb Jones
Page 181...True Focus Photography, Sierra Baker
Page 191...Dave Coverly
Page 209...Shannon Rae
Page 230...Karen Pavone Photography

Appendix photos provided by the author of each section.

Chapter One
A True Story

*If we are facing in the right direction, all we
have to do is keep on walking.*
Jeffrey Goldstein

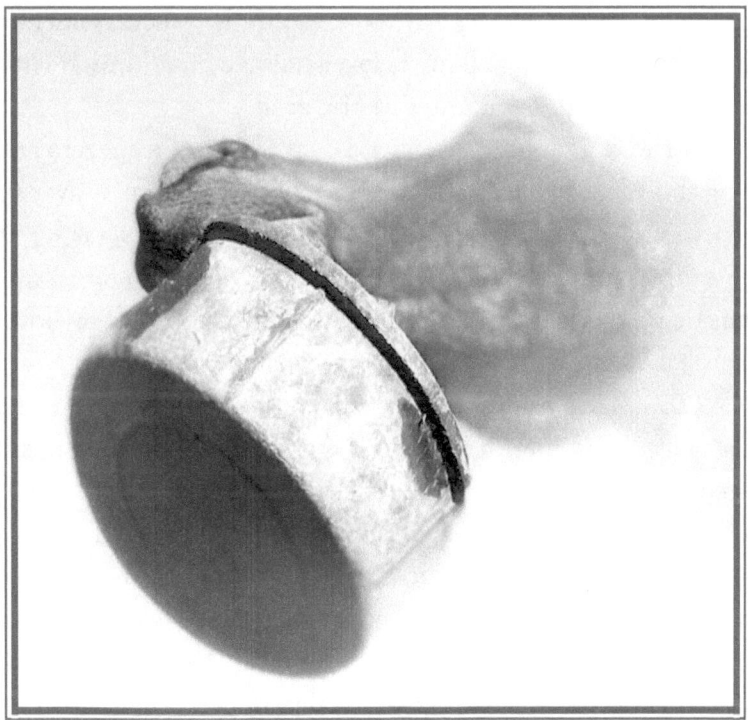

Am I allowed to begin a story with a pandemic?

A story of horses and dogs and cats and life, of how when the bottom fell out of the world as we (thought) we knew it, it fell out of mine, as well? Who wants to read a story about a virus, sadness, uncertainty, hope, love, puppies, and stolen kittens? I'm hoping that you do. It worked for Gabriel García Márquez, as *Love in the Time of Cholera* is one of my favorite books ever. So here goes.

I was cruising along, like we do, kinda fine and just riding around in neutral when everything changed for all of us. It's been so strange, hasn't it? All the cognitive dissonance we've experienced. We stand in this odd place in time our ancestors missed. We have non-stop access to information so we are in a constant struggle to process our shared global environment as well as figuring out what the heck we're doing in our own lives, in our own small place on the planet. As news of the pandemic raced around the world, my own life started gathering up speed, heading way too fast into the valley. Somehow time had caught up with all my beloved animals, and in what felt like a blink, it seemed they were all geriatric or ill.

If I were a biblical character, I'd be Noah. I've got zero ark making skills, but my animal gathering skills are first-rate. Ever since I popped into the world so politely at noon on a Sunday, taking up only twenty minutes of the doctor's time (setting me up for an overly optimistic view of how babies really come into the world) my love of animals has been the framework of what makes me, me.

2021 was a year of great loss all around the world, and in my own small space in the world, too. It was a year marked by much too frequent goodbyes. First to leave us was Clementine, the feral cat who'd found us when we hadn't even realized how shallow our lives were before her. Clem graced us with three glorious years before she was diagnosed with a rare sarcoma which she fought valiantly and with immense courage right until the end. Then we had to say goodbye to sweet Kai, our adopted Golden Retriever who never frowned and had a terrific appetite for Hawaiian Sweet Rolls and any other carbs he could get his paws on. And then, like a hockey hat trick of awful, we had to say goodbye again, this time to our dear little Scout, the tiny terrier who had won our hearts from the moment we first saw him. I was feeling like I'd been hit by every bus on the route when I had to say goodbye to Simba the wonder horse, the rescue who rescued me when he told me, "Ride me," when I had recovered enough to get back in the saddle.

Splat.

My heart had barely recovered from one goodbye before the next one had queued up, ready to rip another hole in my battered heart. I'm grateful for the incredible kindness of our veterinarians; they saw a lot of me last year. In a few short months, everything had changed in the world and in my world. Gone was Clementine's sophisti-cat mastery of everything, from charming serial killer to snuggly lap cat. Gone was Kai's calm Golden goodness, his deep dives into carb loading, and his ever-present smile. Gone was my perpetual shadow Scout, his tiny wise terrier-ness and constant presence. And finally, forming a perfect foursome of heartache, Simba left us, leaving a void where his elder wisdom and his generous soul had blessed us for so many years.

Before you get the idea that I don't care about people, I do, and my own people-loves were taking a beating as well. My hardworking, never-sick mother had suffered a stroke seven years ago, and though we'd initially believed she'd recover quickly both physically and cognitively, she did not. Watching someone you love decline bit by bit is not for the faint of heart.

So, adios 2021; I won't miss ya.

The world was reeling from the pandemic; there was little I could do for my Mom other than be what support I could, and all those goodbyes and losses piled up and weighed heavy on my heart. My four animal partners had been woven into my daily fabric like North, South, East, and West. Those four empty spots in my heart begged the question, "Now what?" Not having animals in my life feels like it's not my life. I grieved, we all grieved, and one day I realized I was ready to begin again. So slowly, bit by bit, I invited new animals into my heart and into our lives. Gone were the days of the quiet understanding the old crew and I had developed. Now everything and everyone was new and we were all adjusting to what that looked like.

Oh, did I mention I hate puppies? Yeah, I kinda do.

Chapter Two
Horsemanship and Life

Horses and life, it's all the same to me.
Buck Brannaman

When my sons were little I realized how little I really knew. Talk about imposter syndrome. Yeah, I'd managed to get myself through college and graduate school twice (don't ask); I was, for all observations, a responsible adult. But being responsible for raising tiny humans? To realize that my role went well beyond ensuring their safety, encompassing not just their physical well-being, but their spiritual and emotional as well? And on top of that, nurturing their unique characters and trying not to stomp on their natural sense of curiosity and wonder? No pressure at all. At the same time I was learning how to bring along a two-year old gelding Skeeter and realizing I wasn't exactly sure how to do that either. Some days I felt like the definition of "fake it till you make it." But the truly beautiful thing about children (and horses) is their willingness to meet us where we are and their tremendous capacity to overlook our failings. It's kind of ridiculous that adults think we're teaching children (or horses) anything, when really, we're the ones who have so much to learn from them. Kids don't care how you look or what kind of baggage you've been dragging around; they see right through you to who you are, the energy you give out, and how you make them feel. Just like horses. And while I was amateurishly trying to figure out how to raise boys and start horses, it hit me, horsemanship and life. Not two separate worlds coming from different parts of me, but one. And it was the same for both; everything I was doing needed to come from my heart.

My sons were teaching me, helping me to see that there were no lines separating the love and the learning, whether with humans or horses. I might not know much, but lead with love? I could do that. The life lessons I was trying to impart, the lessons I was still trying to learn, became woven inexorably with what I was learning in my horsemanship journey. Time-tested basics always applied; set boundaries as solid and helpful as those bumpers at a bowling alley that keep you from throwing a gutter ball, but keep you in the game. Boundaries and expectations that were clear and explained with love, not to exert iron-fist control but designed to allow them to grow in confidence.

I learned the importance of realizing that we are all works in progress and that one set-back doesn't mean we're beyond redemption. Forgiveness is for ourselves as much as it is for others. We can be so darn hard on ourselves. Making mistakes is part of learning, yet when we make one, we want to keep kicking ourselves about it. It took a while but I finally learned that it's healthier to take what we can from the lesson and then put down that stick you use to beat your own head and move on. As my Dad used to say, don't let that one ah sh$t throw out nine atta boys. My Dad's a smart guy. We all have times where we fall below how and who we want to be, when we let anger drive us instead of love, when we act up and out, when we get angry and sad. Or mad. Together my sons and I learned the importance of a true apology; not a coughed out "Sorry, not sorry" but one given with a truly contrite heart when you have done wrong or caused hurt. Over and over I told them that once we've mended fences with a true apology, it's over. I must have made this point very well because many times over the years if I stewed on something they did, they'd say "Mom, you always told us when it's over it's done; move on. Well, you need to move on." Ouch. Truth comes pouring out of children.

Working with horses and raising children may seem like very different things, but I was so grateful to find that life and horsemanship were intertwined in the most beautiful way. My horses and my sons inspire me to be the best human I can be. I'm pretty confident I've always learned more from my kids and animals than they've ever learned from me.

Chapter Three
Clementine's Cat Tales

Synopsis: A sophisticated cat arrived at our house, and turned our dogs-only world into her own.

One rainy day I came home from my new job looking forward to a quiet evening. I'd finally made the decision to leave the job that had left my arms numb for three years. I'm one of those people that stress needs to knock upside the head (or lose feeling in body parts) to get my attention. I'd just thrown my purse down when I heard a loud, insistent meow. We live in the country on a hill and a cat would have to be pretty darn motivated to end up here. I heard it again, and saw a skinny wet cat pressed up against the sliding glass door, meowing loudly for my attention. I opened the door and the poor bedraggled cat rubbed her sodden body against my legs and begged for food. I quickly made up a make-shift meal of dog food and she scarfed it down.

My love for animals could easily run my marriage amok; I could easily be the crazy animal hoarder. Without Pat's wise, ahem, counsel, I'd be the woman with more dogs than you could count, a tribe of goats, a potbellied pig or three, and eighty-nine horses. A hedgehog would be awesome too, and maybe a honey badger. Without Pat to keep an eye on me, my childhood animal gathering skills would kick into high gear. At one point in my eight-year-old life, I had a dog, cat, rabbit, chicken, chameleon, fish, hamster, parakeet, and a snapping turtle. I still wonder what the adults were thinking on that one. My Mom tells a story of my fourth birthday when all I'd asked for was a gray kitten. I didn't get one, but according to her (I'm 65% convinced she made it up) I borrowed the neighbor's gray kitten and they had to physically remove it from my arms. Accused of animal robbery at four, by my own mother.

I hadn't even considered the possibility of having a cat now that I'm not four and old enough to make my own decisions. There's a healthy coyote population around here and it seemed a recipe for disaster. But it seemed there was a cat dispenser dropping wet cats onto our porch. My first instinct was to scoop her up and keep her; that's always my first instinct, if my fourth birthday was any indication. I was afraid sensible Pat would put the hammer down on any adoption ideas I had cooking so I sent out SOS messages to all my cat-savvy friends. She had a clipped ear which meant she was a feral or "community" cat. After hearing that my options ranged from taking her to animal control where she'd have three days to find a new family or else, I started to panic. I couldn't do that. I called Pat and gave him the rundown, already hearing words in my head. No cats. No more animals. We need another animal like we need another kid in college. Do you want a divorce. Stuff like that.

    He listened to my jumbled rush of words and was silent. He was probably figuring out how to tell me no, but nicely, when he said, "We need a cat anyway." Say what? He continued. "She can live in the barn, eat the mice, and it would sure be nice if she caught those @#$% gophers tearing up our lawn." Turns out even after all these years together, I don't know everything about the man. I was grateful we weren't going to have to arm wrestle about her because I was already falling in love. The next day, I took her for a check-up. She wasn't microchipped but it turned out she'd already been spayed in the community cat program. A few tens short of $200 later, and she was turning out to be the best not-free cat ever. Now that it was official, she needed a name. Fortunately, I have a list of names at the ready, with so much breadth and depth I will never run out. We named her Clementine, aka Clem. As soon as Clementine made this her home, the adventures began.

    It's frowned upon to call into work to say you want to stay home to get to know your new cat, so to work I went. I returned, 27 hours after she'd made her first appearance. She wasn't on the back patio where she'd staked her claim and I began to panic thinking we'd only been a temporary stop over on her journey to find a better family. I heard a "meow" and Clementine came running across the yard from over the hill. She was carrying something in her mouth, so I knelt down to pet her and get a better look. Pat had just arrived and came out to see what was going on when she plopped a chubby little rodent at his feet. His nemesis, the gopher. I went inside to get my camera to document the miracle, but by the time I got back she'd eaten the little critter. I'd say she made her vet bill back in good cat deeds. In the span of 27 hours, we'd gone from being a cat-free zone, to a cat-owned family.

Chapter Four
Things Clem Taught Me, or Lessons from a Cat

Love is the great multiplier.
Michelle R. Scully

Kai and Scout weren't sure about this new situation. Clem made herself at home with her new brothers, to their shock and amazement. She introduced herself to little Scout by rubbing against him like, "Hey little dude!" He was flummoxed. She decided that Kai was the guy to cuddle up next to but every time she did, he would get up and move and look at me like I should intervene. Their first conversation went like this.

Kai: (Ignoring Clem, talking to me.) Is this really happening?
Clem: Hold still. I like you, you big goof.
Kai: She's not the boss of me, right?
Me: Remains to be seen bud.

Before long she was lounging around like a tourist at an all-inclusive resort. Our early morning conversations went like this:

Me: Clem, I don't care if you think you're hungry; we do not eat at 4:00 a.m.
Clem: Whatever.
Me: Okay, let me get you some food.

It wasn't long before she owned us. We were all crazy about her. I kept buying cat beds for her, but after cat bed try number five she said, "Still nope. I'll sit next to it, but nope." Before long Clem was managing not only the barn but the house as well; sleeping on our bed, under the bed, and in Pat's sock drawer. I'd go down to the barn to feed and find her standing in the pasture with the horses, or sitting on the salt block, like she was one of the gang. She was my chore partner, but every once and a while she'd go AWOL and I'd hear her meowing to me from the roof of the barn. She knew how to get down, but she preferred me to rescue her. And I was happy to do so. If you'd taken a protractor and swung a big arc, using our house as the center, I'm pretty sure she'd eaten anything not nailed down in that 500' perimeter. We called it the Circle of Death as she'd cleared it so relentlessly of rodents we didn't see a single rattlesnake for years. Since I'd once found a baby rattlesnake (who was pretty pissed BTW) sitting on my desk, that meant a lot to me. Loving a cat must be what it feels like to find yourself in love with a serial killer.

She was sassy, funny, talkative, and magical. All our friends agreed she was a cat of extraordinary character. In fact, most of them tried to steal her once or twice. She sat on the pool table while people were playing, she maintained watch on our retaining wall, just like Jon Snow, to keep an eye out for White Walkers. The miraculous cat dispenser that brought Clem to us scored 100+ points on the match. We didn't know how we'd ever been without her. Life was good, until it wasn't. Last winter, our magical cat had a weird bump that turned out to be a very rare Feline Injection Site Sarcoma, FISS. The diagnosis hit us at the same time as the pandemic. How could this sophisticated cat have found her way to our out of the way porch, only to have a 1:10,000 diagnosis of a rare cancer? What are the odds of all these crazy things converging? When the diagnosis was confirmed, I managed to get off the phone before dissolving into tears. You know the feeling when the thing you dread happens? I phoned Pat, tears coming hot and hiccups of grief breaking my voice. It felt like I got knifed in the aorta. All of a sudden, our magical cat had a nasty, and most likely, unbeatable, battle in front of her. Life is good, until it isn't. Those were gut-punch days, but there were sweet gifts too. When I looked at her sweet little face and heard her purr like an engine, my heart would unclench a bit. My goal was that in spite of this ordeal, Clem would live her best life. And she did, until in spite of all the consultations and efforts we sought, the sarcoma won.

We had three wonderful years with Clementine. Her time with us was much too short, but every day with her was a gift of joy and a blessing. But here's the thing. Any day with the ones we love is a good day. When the sarcoma was at its worst, we were told we had a day, two days at most. But Clem stayed with us for two months beyond that proclamation. She got head scratches as usual, we let her stay out all night if she wanted, she took to walking around on the counters, meowing for cat crack (otherwise known as dry food) at 4 a.m. and I'd jump out of bed to give it to her. Stuff we shut down in the past was just fine. Clem partied all night and slept all day in the laundry hamper, and I'd deliver her snacks deep into the hamper like I was room service and she, an honored guest. Because she was. She made us laugh, she made us smile, she inhabited her body fully. How she ever found us, chose us, is a blessing we will always treasure.

Even in those last days, I learned that no matter what specialists say about a diagnosis, they cannot account for the inner workings of a being; the deep magic of the body and the spirit. I believe when we choose an animal, or by some unexpected blessing, we have the honor of being chosen, part of that privilege is that we need to listen to them when they tell us it is their time to go. And then, we're there for them, every step. No short-cuts. Each day I asked Clem, "Are you okay?" Each day she told me that she was we put in the extra-blessing's column.

I believe animals come into our lives to keep us honest. Humans do some crazy stuff, left to their own devices. We live like we've got all the time in the world; focus on stupid things; worry about things we won't remember in a year; waste time like it's replaceable. Sometimes I wonder if Clementine was sent to help us remember how to live our best lives. I took lessons from her as she lived her best life. I decided I was going to live mine right beside her.

Animals find that space in our hearts that we didn't even know existed, the space they fit perfectly into. When they're gone, that space aches and we believe it will never be filled again. And we're right. That very same space won't be filled. But I believe our hearts and souls are like water, seeking its own level, following the natural law of love. Love is the great multiplier; the more you love, the more you have to share.

We need it, we were designed by love, our souls seek it.

I believe love also seeks us; we just need the eyes to see it, as sometimes it's found in the most unusual places. Just like we learned when Clementine somehow made her way to our back porch; sometimes you don't even know what you need until it finds you.

Chapter Five
Today I'm (Still) Good

Fell off the horse and got back on. It's been a trip y'all.
Michelle R. Scully

  The morning of January 27 I woke up wondering how eleven years had passed so quickly. Eleven years ago I'd gone out for what I thought would be a quick ride with my mare Wish, knowing nothing about how that ride would end and that I'd be facing a new reality by the end of it.
Eleven years is 77 in dog years, if what we're told about dog-time is true. I use Dog Years Math quite often, usually when people

ask how long Pat and I've been married. In case you're wondering, it's been 196. A few years ago we had a big party to celebrate our twenty-fifth anniversary, the end of harvest, and the fact that we hadn't burnt down in the biggest wildfire in California's history the summer of 2018. That fire burned for three months, and our home, our business, our community all had been in the fire's path. It was a gut-wrenching summer. We were all wrung out like sweaty socks. Celebrating twenty-five years was one thing; celebrating what our community had come through the past three months was another. We all needed a party. We served tacos and margaritas and we danced like tired middle-aged people, and somehow that all led to me giving a toast. I shared how many years we'd been married using Dog Math, secure in my ability to multiply 25 x 7, but apparently I can't do basic math once I've had a margarita. Lucky for everyone, numbers are Pat's thing and he isn't afraid to correct my math in public.

    I made myself some coffee as I marveled at how time marches on no matter how hard we hang on to it. All those years had passed since I took that ride which ended in my life-altering accident and the diagnosis my back was so badly broken it would be my own personal miracle if I woke from the complicated surgery able to walk again. I woke from the nine hours of surgery and I do walk, and each year when this anniversary comes around, I remember. This past year has been one of too many goodbyes, of grief, of acceptance, and of starting over. These past two years of the pandemic have made us weary and sad. It's been a lot y'all. I know I'm not alone in feeling like sometimes life lands way too heavy on our hearts.

    I would never have imagined the journey before me; a journey of wreck, wonder, and recovery, filled with lessons learned from horses, dogs, birds, and even cats. I would never have learned the beauty of brokenness; of how letting go of my expectations and in embracing vulnerability, I'd find a new way to live and that new and unexpected life would be so full. I've experienced my own miracles, and on this anniversary I send up prayers of gratitude and am so thankful for my own second chances. In spite of the extensive damage to my spine, in spite of my blown-up L1 vertebrae, through the audacity of my neurosurgeons, the love of my family, and by the very grace of God, I am walking down Buns of Steel hill to the barn, heading towards the horses I'm fortunate enough to be riding again. I can almost feel time drop through the crevices of my hands just like sand, and remind myself once again to live in this moment just like I did with the powerful clarity I experienced after my accident. Eleven years have passed, but the lessons are still the same, and I am still learning them. Breathe. Treasure. Love.

It's rare that any of us end up where we thought we would. Six-year-old me had confidently declared that grown-up me would be a veterinarian, comedian, and a tap dancer. I'm none of those things but I would like to try open mic comedy night one day. I'd buy a round of drinks for the house first, of course. Maybe two rounds.

I'd written this in *Broken*:

"This journey's given a day at a time a new meaning, but that's how I needed to do it. It's how we all need to do it. I had prayed during my anxious nights and finally one morning I woke with words the Lord had put on my heart. He obviously didn't want to overwhelm me with more than four words, and I heard 'Today you're good.' Those few words have become my mantra over these years since, they help me process anxiety and fear into one tiny sentence.

Life.

It's not often what we were thinking it would be, but my heart still feels raw and wide open to the uncertainty and the mystery and the blessing of second chances."

I'm living my second chance, and I never want to forget that. And today, eleven years later, I'm good.

Chapter Six
Just a Mare

The Devil whispered in my ear, 'You're not strong enough to withstand the storm.' I whispered back, 'I am the storm.'
Adharanand Finn

I don't get off what I call "the compound" all that often because it's like a Space-X launch to get all the animals squared away without me. So when I do, it's a big deal. Any chances I get to hook the trailer up and head out, I pack the Cheetos and make the most of it. I'm not sure I can pull a trailer without a bag of Cheetos riding shotgun. I'd headed out for a five- day clinic and was excited to see old friends and meet new ones who share the same passion for horses. Clinic mornings, after we were fed a delicious breakfast (nothing tastes better than food you didn't have to make), were spent around the campfire drinking coffee and talking horses. Life does not get too much better than that.

One morning the conversation ran to mares and why they've gotten a bad rap. Horseman Charley Snell said that back in the day when he was cowboying in Montana, a mare would cost you $50 and a nice gelding around $300. Talk about gender inequality. Working guys had a job to do and their focus was on the job, not the horse. Charley shared that he always bought a mare, for the value, and for the fact that when you were working in tandem with them, they would give you their all.

I loved that. My horses seem always to be mares, which may tell you something about me, and it may not. You don't have to ask around too hard to hear comments like "mares are snarky, they're ruled by their estrus cycle, they have too many (wait for it) opinions." Well, I like my friends to have their own opinions so that's never been a problem for me. One of my childhood friends would never tell me what she wanted to do, so I filled in the blanks as I was never short on ideas, good and bad. Years later she told me how much that had bugged her. I felt blindsided. I asked why she'd never offered up what she wanted to do, and she didn't have an answer. I'm all for telling me anything; good, bad, or ugly, just tell me. Then we know what we're working with.

Mares get a bad deal. I've read that the majority of horses who end up as rescues are mares. The whole PMU (Pregnant Mare Urine, which is used to produce hormone-replacement drugs, is generated by keeping mares pregnant and stalled) industry, breeders who use mares to crank out babies long past when they should—there's a long history of using and abusing mares for what they can do for us. My first horse Pepper was somebody's throw-away horse, but to me, she was a dream come true. She introduced me into the magic of horses. I loved that mare and she spent her last years toting me through orchards and trails. Fast forward to high school and a black mare named Anna. Unfortunately the "trainer" we went to thought Anna had plenty of "opinions" and he was committed to changing them. Not in a nice way, not in a "may I have your thought way," but in a let's run you around till you're too tired to show them way. I look back and feel shame about that. I was young, but still. I wish I had known better. I am so very sorry Anna.

    My journey with mares has continued on. I still have Wish, even after our wreck. It wasn't her fault, or the rabbit's, and I owe her a nice retirement and she's perfectly happy about it. And then, my girl Satin, my second black mare and my comeback horse. I love mares and hate to hear them dismissed as less than or too much. I pretty much just love horses of any kind. We should all be so fortunate as to have a horse with an opinion. Guess what mare-haters of the world? A horse with no desire to show you their thoughts is likely a horse that has had the life and thought snuffed out of them and has turned inward and stoic to be away from that. From us. Give me a horse with an opinion. And if that horse is a mare, let's have some sisterhood solidarity. So mares, bring it. Bring us your thoughts, your curiosity, your heart, your try, your magic. That's the part of horsemanship I love; the learning, the earning of trust, the partnership of it all. If a horse will show me what they think about my part in it, I'm so grateful, because that means I don't have to go searching for them, convincing them it's okay to open up. It means that the life and try within them haven't been dimmed. And if that means that I need to learn more, that I need to get better, that I need to try harder to earn my mare's trust and respect, well, I'm good with that.

The great thing about this clinic, this tribe I've found, is that they all feel just the same. We're in the same boat together, trying to develop our horsemanship and life skills so we can be all we want to be. To our horses, and our people. Looking around the campfire it was easy to make the observation that the clinic was pretty much an all-mare deal. And I'm not talking horses.

Chapter Seven
New Partners

I can make a General in five minutes, but a good horse is hard to replace.
Abraham Lincoln

Have you ever noticed the Universe has more than a bit of an attitude? The last time I'd gone looking for a new partner was when Satin came into my life. Though I have no hard feelings about what happened when Wish and I had our wreck as it was entirely on me, I knew I'd fare better with a new riding horse. Simba had made it perfectly clear that his "Ride me" offer had a three ride cap. He was retired and perfectly happy to stay that way after helping me gather up the courage to swing a leg over again. So I began the search for my new riding partner, and thanks to help from friends, I found Satin.

Satin is my very own Black Beauty; she's been with me eight years. She came from Oregon and helped me get back in the saddle for good. Satin and I've covered a lot of ground together, metaphorically, and literally. She's been a teacher on my horsemanship journey, and a funny one. She's my creeper, or as horseman Josh Nichol explains, a space horse. She can cover a lot of ground inch by slow inch, which has been a great lesson for me. Satin's a quiet character with quite a personality. I've come to describe her as "curious" which is positive reframing in action, because if there's anything to see or get into, Satin's at the front of the line. She can get out of just about any fence, and I've caught her in the barn helping herself to hay when she thinks I'm slacking by not feeding early enough.

Satin's vet file is more than a file; it's what you'd call a dossier. We've been through pigeon fever together, laminitis, lameness, and just to keep things exciting, a rattlesnake bite. She developed a mystery lameness last year and after I'd done the best I could to help pay off the equine lameness specialist's student loans, she was responding well to treatment. I was hopeful we'd be able to ride again. It felt like that hope was well-founded until one morning I walked down to the barn to find her standing like a statue, her front left leg as stiff and big as a tree trunk. I've been spending a lot of time with my vets over the past year, and am blessed by having a remarkable equine vet Dr. Sheri Cronin, who's become a friend as well. I was thinking it was pigeon fever again, but after some detective work Sheri ventured to guess that Satin had been bitten by a rattlesnake. I was floored. Seriously Murphy? Could we get a break on your stupid law for just a bit?

For 72 days I washed, doctored, wrapped, and repeated, as the necrotic action of the venom wrought damage on her leg. Every night Pat would ask, "How's she doing?" and I'd answer, "We'll have to see." Of course, it was the same leg she'd already injured, so it was an actual case of adding insult to injury. My animal partners were gone, my riding partner was out of commission, and it felt like early bird dinner time in Florida with all the old and retired horses around here. Bless Pat's heart, and I mean that in only the best way, not the southern way, but he eventually said out loud what I'd been keeping to myself.

If I ever planned to ride again (and I did, big time), it was time to look for a new horse.

Chapter Eight
Maisy Mae

The face of a Golden Retriever feels like home.
David Rosenfelt

We welcomed Maisy Mae into our family on Father's Day. I tried to convince Pat she was his present, but he wasn't biting. I cried when we picked her up; holding her for the first time stirred up memories of Kai joining our family ten years ago, the sadness of losing him combined with the unbeatable joy of puppy breath.

Yeah, I knew exactly what we, I mean me, were getting into. I know it's almost impossible to believe, but I was the one person in our family saying I didn't want a puppy. But I'm a sucker for a Golden, and though I'd been approved to adopt at the Golden Retriever rescues, turns out they had no dogs. The pandemic had turned people temporarily dog-crazy and for the first time anyone could remember dogs were flying out of shelters; some of them were literally flying as they were being transported from smaller shelters to larger cities. It was a wonderful thing for dogs that needed their own families, and yet a conundrum for us as my heart was set on a Golden. Life without a Golden was well, not golden. They hold a place in my heart, maybe it's their sunshiney personalities, their joy for living, I'm not sure but I love them so. Since there were no rescues to be rescued, it was a puppy for us. I was terrified.

Little Maisy Mae came to be part of our family at the peak of the pandemic while I was working from home, like so many of us. She photobombed about 15 Zoom meetings, chewed on computer cords, and quickly made herself at home. Puppies, like pandemics, turn your life upside down. Both are a good practice in patience, in the importance of naps when it all feels like too much, and in accepting that it's not just puppies that need to learn new things. In spite of spending eighty dollars on chew toys from Chewy.com (I love them, I don't know what I'd do without them) it seemed that the only things she liked to play with were the crumpled up wrapping the expensive toys came in and ice cubes she'd leave on the couch. If you were so unlucky as to sit on one, it looked like you'd wet your pants. That's where turning off the video and using the mute function come in handy. Sometimes I wondered, "Did I really hit mute?" because a few or more swear words might have been said. For months, and about 425 Zoom meetings, I couldn't take my eyes off of her or I'd find her running through the house with my bra in her mouth and 25' of toilet paper trailing after her. Her nickname was Hell on Wheels, for good reason. It's a puppy thing. I know that. But still, some days, it got the best of me.

One night Pat was headed for bed and found me lying down next to Maisy's kennel, all snuggled up with her.

Pat: See, you do love her, right? There's hope?
Me: I've got her in a choke hold so she can't bite my face.
Pat: Sometimes love hurts.
Me: Yea, pretty much every day since this puppy.

Her teeth were shredding machines. I looked like I'd been attacked by a very small man with a very small sharp knife who could only reach my ankles. I spent most my days pulling strange and disgusting items out of the abyss that is Maisy's mouth. One night, I heard her making retching sounds and out came puppy food and a MOUSE. Insert vomit emoji here. They don't call them retrievers for nothing. I started a pile of contraband sticks I'd taken from her and it was literally enough to make a healthy campfire.

There wasn't a piece of turkey poop within a two mile radius that she hadn't snatched up. One Saturday I was convinced I smelled like turkey poop and found out that if you think you do, there's probably a pretty good reason for it. I do bathe regularly but still. It was an awful lot to process on top of world chaos. But there were moments. Moments where I felt a glimmer of hope of who she would be once she lost her razor blade baby Great White shark teeth. The day I found one of those little daggers in my shoe I knew I could hold on. In those rare moments I'd look into those big gray eyes of hers and think yep, we will be best friends someday. I was right. Maisy's growing up now and my arms and legs aren't shredded anymore. I haven't cried myself to sleep while holding her throat in ages. There are moments when she acts more like a big girl than Hell on Wheels.

There's hope for us, I can see the light. Some days I can see a glimmer of who she'll be when her puppy days are behind us if I can just hold on.

Will Rogers said, "If there are no dogs in heaven, then when I die I want to go where they went."

Well Mr. Rogers, I'm fully convinced Heaven is overflowing with dogs.

It's no coincidence that God and dog are made up of the same letters.

Just no puppies please.

Chapter Nine

The Universe is Sneaky,
or
Hello Calamity Jane

I figure if a girl wants to be a legend, she should just go ahead and be one.
Calamity Jane

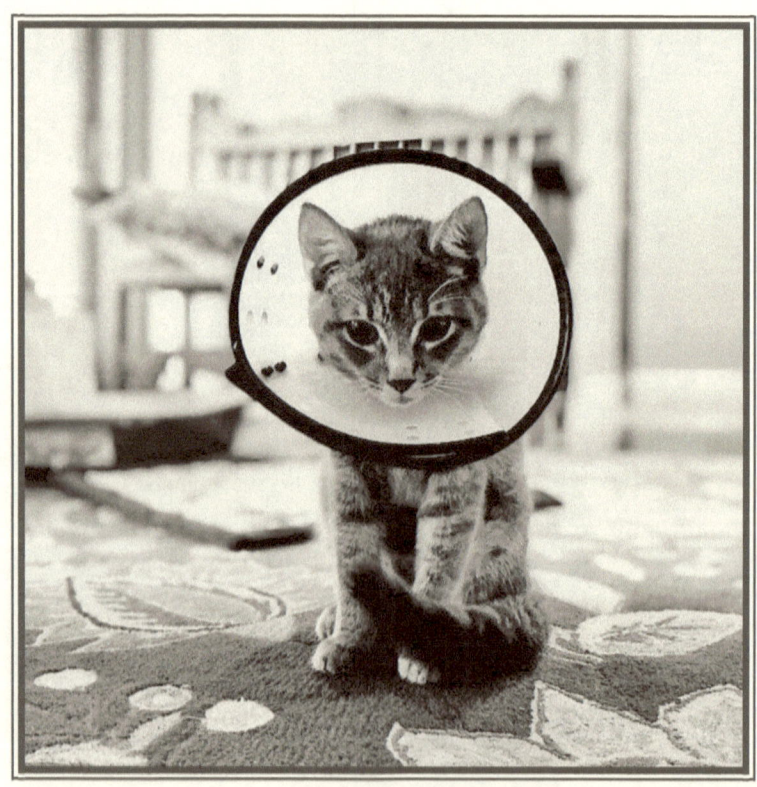

2021 continued to surprise, dismay, amaze, and overwhelm us, flipping all of what we thought we knew a@@ over tea kettle, as the old saying goes. First, when we knew little of how hard the pandemic would hit us all, we were all going shelter in place for two weeks; the next thing we knew, it was two years later. Thank Heaven for animals. Losing Clem had left a huge cat-sized hole in my heart. But she also had left me with the message that I was to open my heart to another cat. She'd proven to us that our family needed a cat to complete the animal farm. To be honest, I wrestled with how that could be? How could I possibly love another cat as all I could imagine was Clem, someone just like Clem, and there's no one like Clem. So what did that even look like? But the big U Universe is sneaky.

A few months later I opened up my heart, took a breath, took a look at all the rescue sites for cats needing homes. It was heart-wrenching. I asked my son Jake if he'd meet me to look at a cat called, of all things, Leslie. Some of my dearest friends are named Leslie, so it seemed like a sign from Clem. Leslie was described as a young adult cat, a brown tabby. Clem was a tabby, something I'd thought little about before Clem, but now I was a tabby groupie so I'd only looked for a tabby just like her. I've learned rescue animal descriptions are pretty much like real estate ads. As the super nice animal shelter attendant went off to get Leslie she said offhandedly, "Oh, by the way, she was scratching at her spay stitches and so now she's wearing a cone and will need 10 days of antibiotics. And she used to have a different name which I won't say, it wasn't very nice because she wasn't what you'd call very nice." I'm glad she couldn't read my mind because I was thinking oh, @#$, great, this will be fun.

She returned carrying a tiny gray kitten-cat wearing a bright yellow cone. I turned to look at Jake and gave him the "uh-oh" look I'd perfected when he was little. This wasn't going anything like I'd imagined. Not at all. This little wanna-be cat was not the right size, not the right color, and I sure didn't need a cat with a cone head. If you're laughing at me right now, go ahead. I deserve it. Like opening your heart up to an animal is something you can control. The attendant left us alone and as soon as she was gone, I told Jake nope, I need to think with my head and not my heart (laugh at me again) and thought, "Pat's not gonna go for this little cat/kitten at all." I was sitting on the floor giving Leslie time to see how she felt about me, and apparently, she thought I was okay as she came over and climbed across my lap. I FaceTimed Pat and introduced him to Leslie, who promptly went up to the camera to say hello. Two minutes later he said, "Yep, that's the one." These girl cats are smart; they know how to win him over—straight out of Clementine's play book.

You'd think I would have learned by now that when the Universe brings a cat into your life, no matter how, you just need to pay Chewy.com a bunch of money and surrender.

And that is how Clementine's legacy brought Leslie, now Calamity Jane, aka Callie, the not-what-I-expected-at-all-but-what-do-I-really-know-about-anything-little-cat-kitten, to become part of our family.

She started out in a box with ten other kittens left on the shelter steps, and now look at her. This little girl who'd been shoved into a box was now riding home with me. It wasn't how I'd been expecting the whole deal to go, but is it ever? It struck me how terrible things can be turned around for good. It was a beautiful reminder in these uncertain times. One of my favorite scripture verses is from Jeremiah and goes, "for I know the plans I have for you; plans to prosper you and not to harm you, plans for a future and a hope."

That's what I want for Callie too.

May she blossom into her full-catness in the warmth that Clem left us as her legacy.

May she be healthy, wise, and only the sweetest kind of serial-killer, and always in charge as only cats can be.

Chapter Ten
The World According to Rufus

If I could be half the person my dog is, I'd be twice the human I am.
Charles Yu

Saying goodbye to little Scout had been gut-wrenching. He'd been my constant companion; I'd been his sidekick for fourteen years. Although our relationship had begun with me under the mistakenly held impression that little dogs were lame; Scout had changed all that for me, and for our whole family. Scout was five pounds of mighty; love, energy, affection, loyalty, all wrapped in a carry-under your arm package of awesomeness. We became immediate converts. And once you've loved a little dog, well, it's unimaginable to live without a little partner. Little Scout was the best dog, big or small, we were so fortunate to have the joy of sharing our lives with.

After the sharpest pain of grief had dulled, we came to the realization that our hearts were ready to look for a little guy. Scout not only had converted me to the little dog way, but he was my first exposure to terriers and well; there's nothing like a convert. So we began looking for a little mixed terrier that needed a family. A few weeks later an ad popped up from a rescue several hours from us. As soon as I saw that little black and white terrier face, it felt like Scout was saying, here, this is the guy.

I felt it in my gut, but the rescue limited adoptions to people within a 45-minute radius. I did some fast math, but no matter which angle of the triangle I looked at, we were well outside that. But that little guy, his little face, kept calling to me. I gathered my gumption and filled that adoption application out with fervor, asked if they would consider us anyway, and pushed send. Then, we waited. Later that evening an email popped up asking if we could schedule a phone call to discuss, and shortly after that I was approved. I was elated. My son Max joined me and we were off to meet the little guy who'd been named Rufus. We loaded Maisy up for her first road trip, and headed down to meet him. We liked him; it seemed like he liked us. When it was time for us to hit the road, his foster people hugged him goodbye, and that's how Rufus came to be part of our family. He's gone from life on the streets of Oakland to going country.

Rufus went country with zeal. He's figuring out country

stuff like cows, horses, deer, turkeys, squirrels, and rabbits. His terrier drive says GO! and he's learning to WHOA. The first week he was here he went tearing off after a turkey and I couldn't believe such a little dog could move so fast. He's full of mischief and smiles and terrier wiles. He's stolen our lunches twice and gets points for strategy. Living on the streets honed his street-smart skills well. I'm pretty sure we fell in love with him on day two. Or one. One. He reminds me of those friends your kids (or you) had—the ones that you're pretty sure might not be the best influence but they're charming and kind and draw you in with such a joy for life that you stop caring about the fact that there's probably a 100% certainty they'll be getting into some kind of shenanigans. You just pray they're not the back of a cop car kind.

He and Maisy are obsessed with each other, making me feel like all the efforts I put into Maisy's puppy training this past year got flushed down the toilet when Rufus won her heart and mind. So, we begin again. Sigh. He's kisses and wiggles, but you can never forget he's got a mouth like a vacuum cleaner and he too thinks the turkeys are leaving special surprises for him on the lawn. He's made his own 10 lb. space in our hearts and I can't help but believe Scout had a hand in bringing us together.

Chapter Eleven
Horse Hunting

The buyer needs a 100 eyes; the seller not one.
George Herbert

Somehow in the crazy chaos of the pandemic, horse prices had skyrocketed. Reading horse sale ads was kinda like reading real estate ads. Every horse was "dead broke" (which is a terrible phrase, really), been there done that, Unicorns, all of them. And the prices, oh my heart. Every day I looked at ads, and every day the prices kept shooting up. My friend Stephanie and I were both in looking mode; we'd share leads with each other and commiserate about whether or not we were willing to sell a kidney to be able to afford a new partner. Some were real true gems, with solid foundations someone had invested time and heart into, and worth every penny. Others were wishful thinking or traders trying to make a buck in a hot market. It was a hard landscape to navigate and more than a little stressful. I didn't want to be looking for a new partner, but I was.

Have you ever noticed that the horse world feels like Six Degrees of Kevin Bacon? I'm amazed at how many people know so many of the same people, all across the country, through something to do with horses. One of my friends had predicted that someone who knows someone would be a lead to find a horse. Commiserating with my vet Sheri about Satin's uncertain situation she'd said, "Oh, we'll find you a horse!" with such conviction I believed her. A few weeks later she sent me a message saying, "I know a horse."

I was so excited to follow up on her lead but we finally were having a spell of real winter weather which kept bumping the date back. Finally, the skies cleared, and it was time to go meet him. You'll be so proud of me—we didn't hook up the trailer the first trip, as I was doing my best to cool my natural impulses and take things slow and easy. That's pretty rare for me, and I'd like points for that.

Remember way back where I asked if you'd noticed that the Universe has a bit of an attitude? Well, it also winks at you occasionally and something really exciting happens. I went to meet that horse and liked him very much.

Chapter Twelve
Hello Handsome

I am still under the impression there is nothing alive quite so beautiful as a horse.
John Galsworthy

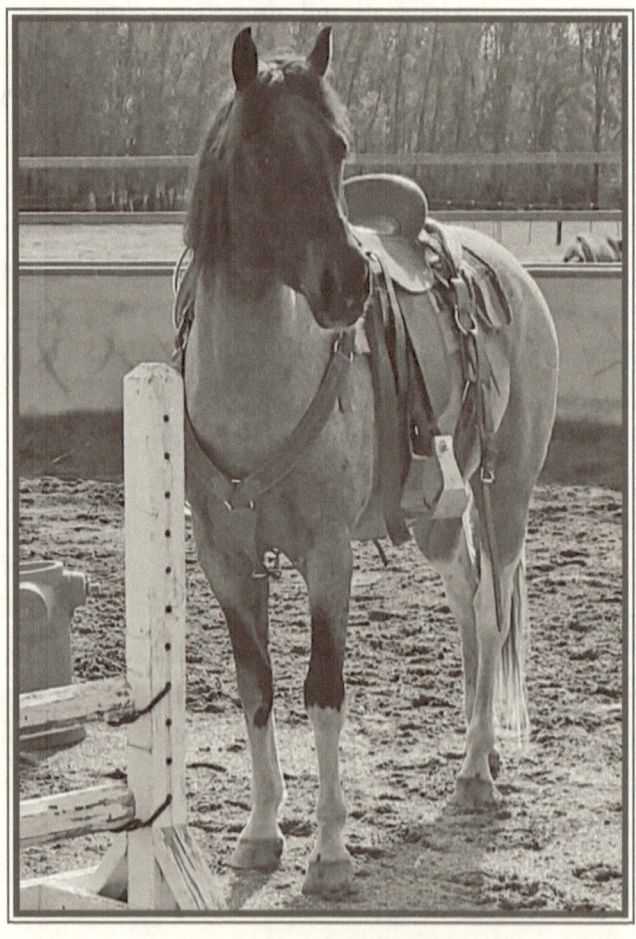

He was described to me as a blue roan, a five soon to be six-year-old, born on Valentine's Day, and consequently, he was named Valentino. I struggled to wrap my head around a horse named Valentino but they called him Little T. Little, because she guessed he was 14.3-ish. Pat offered to come on the drive with me, so we loaded up in the truck and were off. We got there, introduced ourselves and chatted a bit, and finally, there he was. Pat's horse Junior is the size of a moose, so in comparison Little T looked, well, little. I thought his 14.3-ish description was a little enthusiastic, kind of like when I give my height as 5'7." You could measure me all day long up one side and down the other and get a solid 5'6" but there were times I knew for sure that that extra inch was there. You can't blame a guy for slight exaggeration, which does seem to be a guy thing. I'm talking about fish stories of course.

Besides the size situation, Little T looked like a wild child's cookie decorating project. He has a mane we'd all covet. It's a kaleidoscope of color and his dreads would make Bob Marley proud. His head looks like it was dipped in warm milk chocolate, and his body explodes into roan and white and blue and then that wild child poured sprinkles on the rest of him. It was hard to see his chocolate eyes under his fabulous forelock, but they were checking me out as I was checking him out. I'd guestimate his inseam to be 30" if he wore jeans, and I'm used to a guy with a 40" inseam. But when he moved, I sighed. His four white socks (I know the old saying, one white foot—buy him. Two white feet—try him. Three white feet—look well about him. Four white feet—go without him) flash when he moves. He moved like he was floating and he moved like he was ten feet tall. Before long, I'd scheduled a pre-purchase exam (PPE) and the possibility of Little T becoming mine began.

He passed the PPE and you all know what comes next.

Every horse crazy human knows the story of what happens when you hook your trailer up. Little T came home with me. All the discouragement of looking at horse ads and feeling like buying a horse was like buying ocean front property in Arizona was over; of course, we'd all buy anything George Strait was selling, but that's a different story. I'd found my guy, or he'd found me, and our journey together and all that was to be, was now riding home in the back of my trailer.

On the drive home, I thought about names, and life, and the journey we're all on and "True" came to me. I decided I was calling him True and by the time he was unloaded, that's who he was. True, like true north, towards seeking, and becoming, your best truest self. It felt right, like it summed up the impetus behind my horsemanship/life journey. It suits him, and feels really good to me.

It's a nerve-wracking moment when you're finally ready to unload and open that trailer, as you're really opening the door to a brand-new relationship with all your hopes and dreams attached. This isn't my first rodeo with a new horse, but I'd grown so much in my horsemanship journey in the eight years since Satin had come to be with me. I was excited to start our relationship. I wanted very much to begin it with no expectations beyond my own investment that I would do all I could to be a good partner to him. I was excited to learn about him; what he knows, what he doesn't, and about the new journey we will have together. We'll take the time it takes to build good things together.

We unloaded. He shook his bodacious mane and readjusted himself, ready to meet the girls next door. Next to the girls it seemed as if his 14.3 was wishful thinking for sure, but what he lacks in cannon bone length he makes up for in all around fabulousness. If he were a cake donut, he'd be one with chocolate frosting and rainbow sprinkles. I'm pretty sure if I tried really hard, I could fit him in my purse. In spite of old man Sundance trying to kick the fence down last night (who'd have thought that octogenarian had it in him?), he settled down pretty well.

Day one, going in the win column.

Welcome True. Off we go.

Chapter Thirteen
Animal Farm

Some people talk to animals. Not many listen though. That's the problem.
A.A. Milne

If we all had to wear name tags to describe ourselves, mine would say "Hi, my name's Michelle, and I love animals." Pat calls my crew of animals my animal farm. He has a point; two dogs, five horses, one cat and an auxiliary crew of wildlife make up the farm. There are a lot of names to remember around here, not even counting all the nicknames everyone has. Sundance, Wish, Satin, Junior, and True make up the five-horse herd. Maisy Mae and Rufus for the canine crew, and Calamity Jane represents the cat contingent. It only takes one cat to make up a contingent, that's for sure. Each year I ask for goats for my birthday, but somehow that never happens. We have a rotating herd of cattle that comes here in the spring, although this year's group is pretty lackadaisical about their job. I give them a B-/C+ in Grazing.

That's just the domesticated part of the animal farm. Daisy and Oliver the raven couple are also on the payroll. I buy them special food and they aren't above helping themselves to it if I forget to close the tack room door. They also aren't shy about having conjugal visits in front of me and they're pretty good at it. One year they had three babies, the Tres Amigos, who were such a handful I think I was just as glad as Daisy and Oliver were when they took them off to live on their own. This year they only had Baby Uno, who was adorable and much more polite. There's also what Pat calls the Deer Farm; about 800,000 deer, give or take, who wander through our barn, helping themselves to whatever looks delicious and sharing meals with Sundance if he lets them. Each morning a pair of sweet Black Phoebes sit on the fence by the house, flicking their tails and singing their distinctive tee-hee tee-hoo song. Last year they decided to build their nest on top of the light in the tack room. I couldn't close the door or turn on the light for weeks. Finally, one day four big-mouthed faces peeked out over the edges, chirping madly at me as if I were their derelict mother. A mama gray squirrel tries to keep track of her three juvenile delinquents as they run and tumble over our patio furniture giving her a fit. A beautiful pair of osprey fly overhead each morning on their way to breakfast on the lake, and every once in a while a stately Great Blue Heron graces the hills, still as a statue, patiently waiting.

Since I've started working from home, I see more of the animal farm than I do people. Some days I miss feeling a part of a group of people working on a project. Some days I miss wearing actual outfits rather than the same uniform of one pair of jeans worn over and over. But most days, the animal farm keeps me company and is never boring. Finding someone to watch them all when we leave isn't easy. No denying they're a handful, but it's worth it to me.

Though I take care of the domesticated animals, I'm only an invested observer to all the other wildlife here. Through them I have a bird's eye view of the ever-changing canvas of nature, the shift of seasons, the ebb and the flow of life. In observing them I learn the cycles of the day, of their lives. Each day is the same in some ways; ever-changing in others. In the quietness of time spent without human company to chatter to, I too can sink into the timeless pattern of nature. I watch the daily patterns change around me, watch the animals both tame and wild responding to the subtle changes in daylight, inexorably drawing them into one season and leading them out of another. I feel as if I, too, can sense the small changes in the days as we all make our 365 day orbit around the sun. I'm just an observer, but somehow this vantage point feels as if it binds me to the earth, in ways being indoors never could. We've lost touch with that connection to nature, I think, insulated as we are in buildings with artificial light and temperature at our fingertips.

We fall asleep to the coyotes howling at the moon, calling to each other in the privacy of night. Sometimes they're obnoxiously loud, but the nights would seem strangely empty without the occasional coyote cacophony. They too are part of it all. Life in the country makes me happy. I feel blessed to have a front-row seat to see such tender parts of life; watching the does bring their tiny spotted fawns down from the hills, Daisy and Oliver showing off their noisy babies to me, and finally, watching as they take them out into the world to be on their own. Nature is a sublimely beautiful artist and a harsh taskmaster. The unstintingly terrible is just as much a part of life in the country; the harsh reality of death is constant. The cycle of life is filled with both sweet moments and hard goodbyes. But this life I have, surrounded by animals living life as only they know it, hits me deep in the marrow of my bones and suits me well. I feel blessed to experience the all of it.

Wherever you go there you are there you are,
there you are
between the gravel and the sky all the highs and all the lows
between the sunset and sunrise
being young and getting old
between the coming and the going
the learning and the knowing
I'm thankful for these wild and wondrous days
I get to keep
Living between the hat on my head
and the boots on my feet

Boots on My Feet, by Drew Kennedy

Chapter Fourteen
Begin at the Beginning

Every new beginning comes from some other beginning's end.
Seneca

True's been here 10 days now. Each day we see and do new things. We spend some time in the round pen but I'm not chasing him around it. Been there, done that, done with that. I'm grateful to the horsemen and women over these years who've helped me to see there's a better way.

A way where the horse's peace of mind matters. One based on a foundation that recognizes how vital it is to have the horse's thought, that works to keep that "cup of worry" horseman Harry Whitney describes empty, and one that provides a horse the freedom to make a choice. This is the kind of foundation I'm seeking to build with my horses. It's different and it asks a lot of you, but when you see it, you see what a beautiful difference it is.

I've been taking a deep dive into what choice looks like in my horsemanship. I can't think of a better opportunity to do so than now in starting this new relationship with True. I'm grateful to horsemen Warwick Schiller and Josh Nichol for the incredible discussions they're both having about what this looks like with our horses. I'm grateful for their openness in sharing their own horsemanship/life evolution and journey. True looks at me as if to ask, "Okay lady, how're we going to do this? What do you want from me?" That's a fair question. This time I'm taking a different approach, one that I'm only just learning about, and trying to translate to True. I think it's different for him too; so we begin together.

I ask True, "Can you be here with me?" working with the smallest of asks. Asking for his thought, for his mind, to be with me rather than off in the hills or anywhere but here. He's curious, wondering what the heck I'm doing, but willing. His ears are like antennae, at the ready, scanning his environment and reporting back. He moves his head toward me, but his eyes are still looking off to the side so I ask him again. "Hey buddy," I think in my head, trying to convey this in silence but with intent. His eyes lose their locked down look and flash to me. "Hey buddy," I say again, still silently but with a big smile on my face. That's it True; that's all I'm asking for. You. Me. Here. Together. He gives a big sigh, a lick and chew, and I think I do, too. Off we go!

And I keep trying to feel this out. How it looks to ask, rather than dive in and grab it, which I'm coming to realize I've done way more of than I thought I had. Simple things, or so I thought. You just go get your horse, right? Grab a halter, go get your horse, and off you go? Oh, dang, I'm realizing there's so much more to that. I'm learning, slowly, but learning, that even the so-called simple things speak loudly to horses. When I go to halter him, I ask him to come to me, to offer me his head, rather than chasing after it.

It can be pretty dang hard to be more compelling than the two mares, that's for sure. True does like the girls. But it's exciting and challenging, and when I get those "yes-es" it's pretty darn intoxicating. His choice to my question; it's a beautiful thing. Each day he says yes more quickly than the day before. And then, some days he doesn't, but I stay the course. There's a lot to see outside the fence; the other horses are interested in him and he in them. He's in a new world and it's on me to provide the support and relationship he needs to confidently grow and learn and become all he can be.

This is my journey too. True's not the only one who has much to learn. Long ago, I learned that I have way more to learn than he ever will. I'm okay with being a perpetual student. I'll make mistakes; I'll regroup; I will try again. I'm focusing on the relationship we're building rather than becoming stuck on getting a particular reaction. The one thing that doesn't change regardless of his response is my goal and desire to be calm and supportive no matter what or where. Do no harm, try a new way, or try again, becomes my mantra. As my friend and amazing horseman Mark Rashid once told me, as long as mistakes do no harm, then what's the harm in making them? Mark's a smart guy. Some days I'm just hanging out in the sun with this little roanie pony. And he's pretty cute, isn't he?

Relationship making. It feels really, really good. Uncharted, but good.

Chapter Fifteen
Do the Work

Before the inside of the horse can be right, the inside of the person needs to be right.
Tom Dorrance

One of the things that's been most transformative in my horsemanship is right here, in this chapter's quote.

It's impacted how I see my relationship with my horses, my part in it, and in the people I choose to learn from. If we're frustrated, angry, or afraid to try for fear we'll get it wrong, it's pretty darn hard to show up for our horses in the way they need us to. I love how Josh Nichol's horsemanship incorporates how our inner life is intimately connected to our relationship with our horses. How we can take care of our needs so that we can see and meet theirs. It's good stuff.

We need to do our work, before we "work" our horses.

I'm working on it.

Chapter Sixteen
Making a Horse From the Inside Out

Training a horse is mainly about feeling and trying, according to what we feel, to help, and not force.
Nuno Oliveria

Remember when...we called it breaking horses?
Ouch.
And then, we started calling it training horses. I still struggle

with that. Maybe it's semantics, but I think for me it's an effort to break away from a history where training was something done to horses to get an end result, not about how or what getting there looked like.

There was a time starting a horse hard and fast was the norm, and unfortunately, it's still being done today. Thankfully, our language has shifted from "breaking" to "training." But I still struggle with "training." I've kinda fallen on to "making" a horse. Not "training" a horse, but "making" a horse (and its human). We go looking for a horse with a list of descriptors we want. Big horse, tall horse, short horse, paint, roan, gelding, no mares for Heaven's sake, 12 years old, two years old, not too old, not too young. We don't often look inside of them. We go looking with a framework of what we like in terms of looks, a price point, and then we look for the horse that meets those external characteristics. We don't seem to ask horses "will you be mine?' or, "may I be yours?"

Smart horsemen look beyond that; they look at the eye, the try. Even smarter ones look at the heart. They see things that those of us who are still a little bit behind them on the journey often miss in the overwhelm of searching for a new partner. But we forget that choice component—just because we got them, bought them, doesn't make them ours or us theirs. That's the relationship part; making a horse from the inside out, not the outside in.

With all that we've learned (slowly, so dang slowly, we humans can be so dang SLOW to get it, but still we're getting there) what should we call it?

>A horse maker
>A horse shaper
>A horse learner
>A horse listener
>A student of the horse?
>Yeah, I like that one.
>A student of the horse.

Sign me up for that.

Chapter Seventeen
Stupid Horses

If given a little thought, a little understanding, and a little common sense, the horse gives back in full measure. If the human can give 5%, the horse will come from the other side with 95%. The horse never ceases to amaze me with what he can get done with very little help from the human.
Ray Hunt

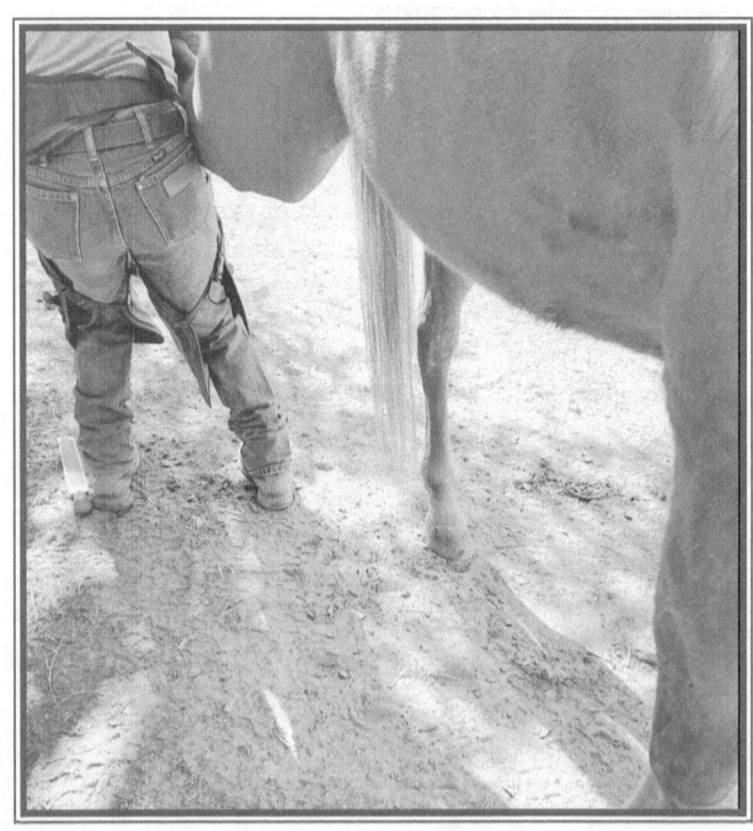

Horses are anything but.

Last week my awesome farrier Jeff was out to do everyone's feet. Sundance is by far the oldest guy here, and he's pretty much just eating lots of expensive special food and enjoying the sunshine in his well-deserved retirement. It's easy to overlook the old guys, those that aren't bursting with youth and energy. And yet, every time it's Sundance's turn, I'm moved by how he responds.

Each time Jeff would move, Sundance would shift his weight, lift his foot, and wait.

It was such a thing of beauty it brought tears to my eyes.

Ray Hunt said, "The horse is a thinking, feeling, decision making animal, but the human always acts superior. The human thinks he's smarter, he always wants to have things his way, and right now. He wants to be the boss. If trouble comes up, he turns it into a contest with the horse. What I'm talking about developing with the horse is not dominating by fear, but more like dancing with a partner.... The kind of dancing where his body and your body become one."

I saw that dance this morning, the dance of the feet, and let me tell you, it was a beautiful thing.

We're the ones who need the dance lessons.

Chapter Eighteen
New Boy in Town

Everybody's talking 'bout the new kid in town.
The Eagles

Never underestimate a short guy. True landed in town and the girls knew it. He did not land lightly but with a thump. They were checking him out; he was checking them out so nonstop that by the second morning he was here I went down to feed and found him on their side of the fence. He may have a career in jumping; I don't know.

The girls found him irresistible and from the looks of what he was flashing, (yes, I do mean flashing) it was obvious he felt the same. Very obvious, to the extent I had to stop to make sure I had indeed brought a gelding home because he seemed anything but. As a freshman at UC Davis, I did what all typical horse-crazy girls do and sought out an internship at the horse barn. Essentially, my internship consisted of cleaning out long-forgotten stalls and teasing the stallions. If you don't know what that means, look it up. That was an eye-opener. I mean that literally, my eyes were as big as soccer balls at some of the things I learned. Pure animal instinct in action can be intense. I hope I don't have to spell this out for you. If you're scratching your head, go read Everything You Ever Wanted to Know About Sex but Were Afraid to Ask, Animal Husbandry edition.

As chaotic as things were due to True's too-sexy presence, this is not my first rodeo. In fact, it's probably my 462nd rodeo. But it was definitely one of the more exciting rodeos. It wasn't even spring time when thoughts normally turn to love, but the girls immediately went into big-time heat. They'd also done that when Junior arrived, but this time was extra-extra; like Junior-on-steroids. Satin and Wish had been swooning over the sheer manliness of Junior when he first arrived, but he's a big horse walking around sporting a 40" inseam while True is a 30" at best.

No disrespect to True's height because apparently, he's putting the "lit" in little.

Chapter Nineteen
My Hindsight's 20/40

Get in over your head, as often and joyfully as possible.
Alexander Isley

Disclaimer: I didn't *fall* off Wish in the case of my unfortunate dismount. I bailed off. There is a difference, but unfortunately, the result was the same. In the heat of the moment, it seemed like a good idea. But in hindsight, um, not so much. In my mind, I saw myself doing an impressive mid-air dismount and landing gracefully on my feet. No, I wasn't drinking and riding, but somehow in the chaos of the moment it had sounded like a good idea. The dismount, not the drinking.

It wasn't.

But what's new? Unfortunately, I'm not alone in this. We've all done things that seemed right in the moment, but after? Well. We all have a list of things we wish we'd done differently. They say hindsight's 20/20 but mine's probably a solid 20/40, some assistance required to see clearly. We all wear a type of vision correction, things that impact our ability to see what's before us without emotion, fear, anxiety, or anger coloring it. It's not easy. We all have triggers, and when those triggers get stacked up, our circuits can overload and we can make less than stellar decisions. It's the same for our horses. When something frightens them that fear can activate their sympathetic nervous system where flight and survival override their "everything's chill, life's okay" parasympathetic nervous system. I'm grateful that in hindsight I can see what went south when Wish and I met the rabbit, which set into motion all the things that went wrong before the big thing went wrong. Wish had told me very clearly when something in the environment grabbed all her thought, and I ignored it. In our case, the things that went wrong were there, and I overlooked them in my desire to get home before dark.

Since *Broken, Tales of a Titanium Cowgirl* was published, I've talked with many people who've had a wreck of one sort of another, and I know not everyone knows what went sideways. That's a tough one. That introduces uncertainty and erodes our confidence when we do desire to get back in the saddle. That erosive feeling is a tough one to combat, but maybe combating it isn't the answer? Maybe giving ourselves permission to question it, to feel angst about it, to try to unravel it to find any hidden clues is the first step in healing rather than "cowgirling up" and getting back in the saddle even when everything in your being is silently screaming, BUT I'M AFRAID. Maybe, rather than hide the fear, or fake it till you make it, maybe we could grant ourselves grace and permission to make that walk back step-by-tiny-step if that's what it takes. Yeah, the old adage is "if you fall off a horse, get right back on" but I say good riddance to that old rubbish.

We need to understand *why* we came off, from our perspective and from our horses' perspectives. It might take time; it might take a lot of time. Oftentimes, there are clues and it's important we discover what they were and what led up to them. Crazy wrecks do happen, as my sweet friend Beverly could tell you when she and her good boy rode over a yellow jacket hive. Things like that can and do happen.

There are many post-accident scenarios. It's so easy to feel overwhelmed. You may decide you're never getting back on. You may decide that you want to spend more time on the ground with your horse until you feel like throwing a leg over. There's plenty you can do with your horse without being in the saddle. Make up games, play soccer, look for squirrel holes and fill them with rocks, ride your bike around the field. If these suggestions sound oddly specific, well, that's because I've done them all.

Sometimes it just takes the time it takes. The arm-chair quarterbacks of the world like to tell us what timetable we should be on. Emphasis on should. There are all kinds of time zones, and what works for someone else may not be your best time zone. When you've had a traumatic experience with a horse, the aftermath can feel like a very lonely place to be. It needn't be. I don't want it to be that for you. That's the reason I wrote *Broken, Tales of a Titanium Cowgirl*. There are many of us out there who've ended up in a place we didn't expect to be. Unfortunately, it's not an exclusive club. It's a club I don't wish anyone entre to, but if you are a fellow member, then please know you have company. You are not alone, and there's an odd comradery in sharing that with other horse lovers.

Give yourself time.

That was the hardest and best lesson I learned.

Apply an extra dose of grace.

When it seems like just too much, breathe. It's amazing how that helps.

Get some purr-therapy from a cat.

Pet a dog.

Sit in the sun.

You can do this. I'm cheering for you. xox

Chapter Twenty
A Place of Neutral

When your horse is relaxed, mentally with you, their mind is in neutral, they are like butter on a plate on a warm day.
Charley Snell

True and I are getting to know each other, working on small things. Small things, we often learn the hard way, are often really the big things, or the building blocks of the big things. They're usually not sexy things, so we tend to speed by them or ignore them. Often to our own "oh crap how'd I miss that!" realizations when we find out (as we always do) that they were indeed really important. In his book *True Horsemanship through Feel* horseman Bill Dorrance says, "little problems people ignore lead to bigger problems they can't ignore."

One of the biggest things we're working on is being together, mentally. I've been thinking about what one of my favorite horsemen, and dear friend, Charley Snell, says about "a place of neutral." A place of neutral is when your horse is turned loose, physically and mentally, their thoughts present with you. It sounds so simple, but so many horses and their humans have never really spent time making this a priority.

What does having a horse "mentally with you" even look like? It's something that once you experience it, you wonder how you ever missed it. It's a place where you're asking your horse to be here, with you, no matter what the two of you are doing. From haltering to picking up a rein. As Charley says, he never indiscriminately picks up a lead rope or a rein. It's done with purpose, in asking for the horse's thought.

Asking, offering, for them to be with us physically and mentally in a relaxed state of mind. When you find that spot together, I'm pretty sure anything is possible. True was in neutral, and as I left, he was in drowsing in the sun mode. His girlfriend (one of them) Wish keeping an eye on him from afar. It's probably just me, as we humans love to anthropomorphize our socks off, but I coulda sworn he was smiling. It's a beautiful thing, and I'm grateful for it. I'd swear True is too.

Chapter Twenty-One
Have a Heart

*Every horse has a heart. If we were to think more on this, perhaps our
relationship with them would be better.*
John Saint Ryan

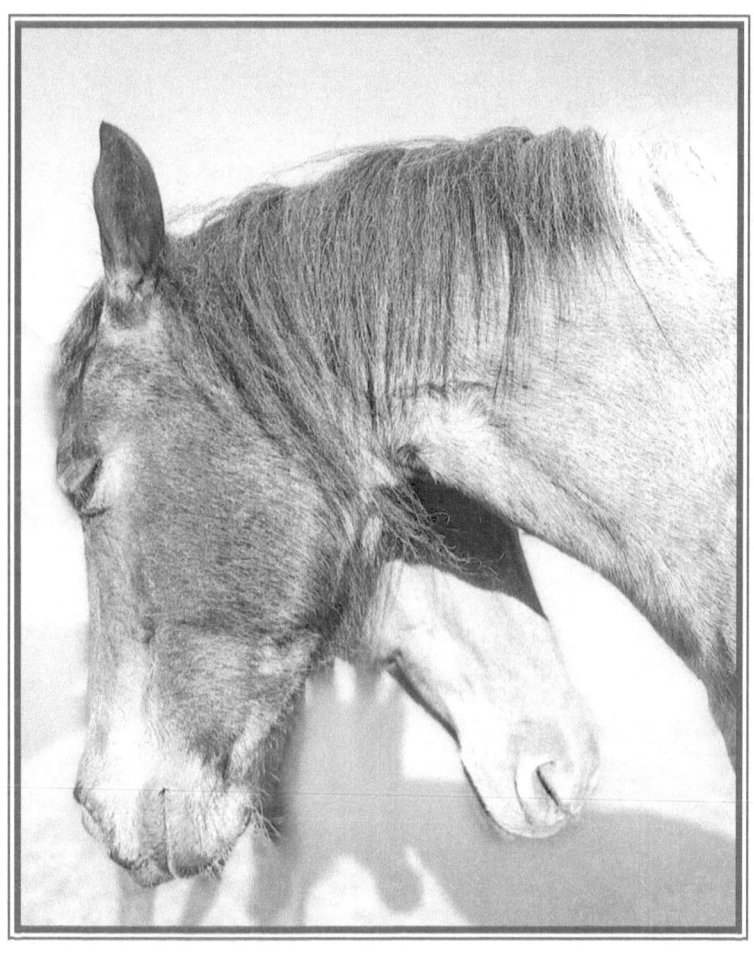

Some wise horse people are focusing on building relationship over agendas with horses and it's helping to change the landscape from how things have been done in the past.

Things as simple and common sense like:

Respond to your horse as you'd like them to be (same goes for unruly people I'm thinking....).

Be the kind of partner you'd like to be paired up with.

Say thank you.

Try kindness.

Do everything with good intent.

Believe in your horse so your horse can believe in you (Mr. Ray Hunt).

I love this quote, from the ever-wise John Saint Ryan, to encourage us to recognize that every horse's heart is special.

Chapter Twenty-Two
Inner Life

It never hurts to keep looking for sunshine.
Eeyore

Zero complaints about the rainy weather we're finally having. The thirsty trees are so grateful after so much drought. Yesterday it was dry enough to try a horse introduction. It's been challenging figuring out who can go with whom now that there's True, who thinks he's the new sheriff in town. Turns out he is all about the mares, and he and giant Junior are not simpatico. Imagine two bears meeting for the first time and the small one thinks it's a perfectly fine idea to poke the big one. That's True and Junior. My mixed herd's worked in the past but as we know, every day, every situation is dynamic with horses. In spite of all my good intentions, introductions turned into a bit of a dust-up.

Not gonna lie, I was feeling pretty discouraged. Life is a LOT easier when everybody gets along. Horses and people. Adding all the new animals to my life this year was evoking lots of change and added responsibility on my part. It's been kind of overwhelming having all these newbies at once. Finally, I got everybody shuffled back to where they'd been and headed to the house with my tail between my legs to regroup and make some tea. Tea fixes a multitude of sins. Wine on the other hand, well, not so much. This was on me; I was missing something. True's behavior with the ladies was on steroids, but I was interpreting it as chaos that would last forever. When I stepped away from my emotions, thanks to the tea (it was the Brits that coined Keep Calm and Carry On) I could see the troubles were stemming from how True was feeling inside. No doubt he was feeling uncertain in his new home and finding his place in things.

I finished my tea, dusted myself off, and went out into the pasture with a smile plastered on my face in fake-it-till-you-make-it mode. I was committed to shooting peace, calm, and imaginary glitter all over that pasture. Go figure, Satin came right up and stood by me, leg cocked, relaxing in the sun. Then Wish. Moments later, True came over and lay down nearby. It worked! I was so excited I fist-bumped my own self. All the horses needed to feel safe and calm in the face of all the recent changes, and once I let go of my emotional interpretations, I was able to be that place for them.

When circumstances tie a knot in my tail, I remind myself, every day's a new day.

To learn more, to try different things, to change things up. What is now isn't for always. It's so easy to forget that.

Chapter Twenty-Three

A Place of Peace

*The horse is a mirror.
It goes deep into the body.
When I see your horse I see you too.
It shows me everything you are, everything about the horse.
Ray Hunt*

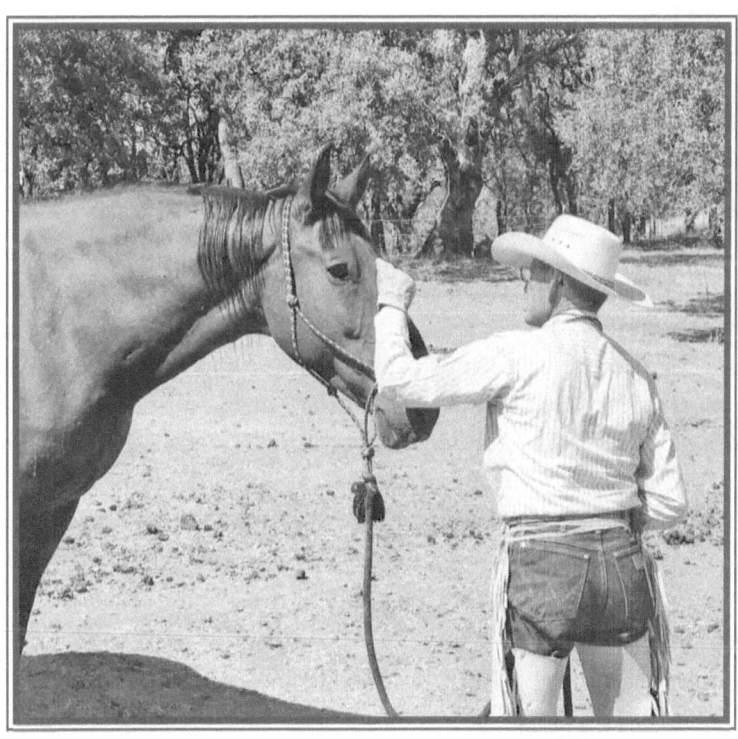

If you're looking for tips on shoulder in, this will be pretty darn disappointing.

I was excited to be hosting a four-day horsemanship clinic with my friend Charley Snell. I'd met Charley a few years back at a Harry Whitney clinic. I was sold on Charley as a horseman and human when he helped me so much in just a short walk about with Satin with his knowledge and his kindness. Charley'd agreed to come down our way to put on a clinic and it was as good as I'd imagined. By the end of the fourth day, my head was feeling pretty full. So much to learn, and such a wonderful teacher.

Sitting together in the morning sharing a cup of coffee and horse thoughts, talk turned to how horses feel in new environments. We all have stories that start with "my horse does fine until..." or, "my horse isn't comfortable in new places...." Charley put on his serious face and shared what he believes is the key to all this. That the horse looks to us for a place of peace.

Us.

Charley's a wise guy, in the best kind of way. "Any little thing you can do to help the horse feel good inside adds to this whole thing," he said. "It's not about a different environment or a change in scenery. It's about how we help them feel *no matter what's going on, no matter where they are*." It really comes into perspective when you think about how looking to you when things get dicey becomes particularly vital on a narrow mountain trail. Horses by nature are all about self-preservation. It's the essence of them, and incumbent upon us to recognize and honor this truth. How vital it is to recognize and be responsible for taking good care of the horse's spirit and sense of preservation. And of what a difference it makes in our relationships when they feel that from us; feel safe from us and with us.

I love that. Rather than thinking, "how do I get this movement to happen," to focus on, "how can I help my horse feel better about what we're doing?" I'd never heard any of this when I was first around horses. I had no idea how much my horse wanted to feel safe, to feel good. This relational aspect of being with horses needs to come from us. That's the challenge and the blessing for those of us who love horses. That's within our part of the relationship. Us, supporting the horse. If they don't feel it from us, they won't choose us.

As we sat there soaking it up, wondering what this would look like, Charley helped us out with the perfect words; a horse that is mentally present. Relaxed. Alert. I scribbled his words down in my notebook and underneath all my jottings I wrote, "My Goal: Be that place of peace."

Chapter Twenty-Four

Wait for It

When the horse finds we will wait on him, what a profound effect it has.
Charley Snell

Charley shared these words at the clinic I was hosting, and they hit me upside the head. Wait. Please no. Thanks a lot, Charley. We're really bad at waiting. Well, most of us. Okay, well, me. Sorry I tried to lump you in there, too. I hate waiting. In horses and in life so many things are designed around a quick fix and "Buy this ____ and all your dreams will come true" promises. We want it now, thank you very much. Instant gratification feels so good, and the emotional part of our brain wrestles with the logical part of our brain to choose it. Broccoli or cake? Enough said. We've also got that sneaky human agenda issue going on; what we want to do and on our timeline. With horses we've learned we're supposed to ask, but if we don't get the response we're expecting right away, it's so easy to start escalating. If we're honest though, it's not really an "ask" if we demand it. My default mode is, "Here let me help with that," but I'm learning that helping isn't always helpful. It's just so darn tempting to help it along, pushing things to happen before they're ready to happen. But by overlooking our horse's effort and not allowing them the time to search, we can shut down their curiosity and the try in them. Why try if you're not ever going to be right?

Waiting feels like a lost art. My grandparents' generation was forged in the Depression-era and they knew how to wait. How to look down the road and hang in there for the long-haul. My grandparents had every rubber band off every newspaper they'd ever read, just in case. I wish I had about 100 of them right now. Fast forward a couple generations and we're almost hard-wired for NOW. Charley said he's missed many suppers because he was into something that required wait. And wait he did. Till supper got cold.

It's always one thing to hear it, another to see it. The day was drawing to a close and the late-afternoon sun streaming into the arena bathed Charley and the horse he was working with in a golden glow, cocooned in a time bubble where only the two of them mattered. We all watched quietly and finally were able to feel what he meant by wait. There was no rush, no escalation. It wasn't "Hey, let's take a nap" waiting. The time he offered her felt expectant and hopeful. His hands lifted the lead, they gave her a feel to follow, and then he waited for her to find it. It was such a beautiful thing when she did.

This was a lesson I needed. In horsemanship, and life. Life's too short, that's for sure, but that doesn't mean we need to rush through it.

We don't notice enough of the good things he (the horse) does and while he's doing those good things, we just take them for granted.
We do way too much physically.
Ray Hunt

Chapter Twenty-Five

Blind Date

Single, want to mingle?
Um, no thanks.
Michelle R. Scully

There's something about a single friend that screams, "Set them up!" Before I was married for 196 Dog Years, friends loved to say, "I know the perfect person for you!" Of course, I loved my friends and assumed their pickers were infallible. I mustered up my courage and agreed to a blind date; we made plans to meet for a drink at a restaurant. No red carnations were worn, but we found each other anyway and sat down to chat.

Sigh. The guy was a golf pro and immediately started talking about birds but in golf language. Now I love birds but I don't know the difference between a birdie, an eagle, an albatross, or a turkey. Most importantly, I don't want to. The only thing I like about golf is the outfits because plaid is totally awesome. He kept talking about golf while my eyes got heavy and my 8th grade nervous tic of yawning uncontrollably returned. I looked longingly at my cheap glass of Chardonnay and considered gulping it down in one shot. Not too long into our meet and greet I made semi-polite excuses and got out of there. It only took me two blind dates to realize that while friends have only good intentions, bless their hearts (southern sarcastic), what they were seeing wasn't potential compatibility but, "You're both single, you should mingle. And then get married, of course."

One day I had a flash-back to those awful blind dates and when I was done retro-actively cursing my friends I thought about True and the relationship we're building. Because I can make literally any thought (especially golf) turn to horses. I thought it's like a blind date in a way. Poor horses! We begin new relationships with new horses thinking I WANT A HORSE, while the horse is busy being a horse. We come in hot and fast, decide this is the horse for us, load him or her up, and off we go. HAHA! YOU ARE MINE, we think, gleefully driving that trailer home loaded with all our hopes, dreams, and expectations. We plop them out and say, "You're mine now; let's do this thing." It's no wonder so many horses have anxiety.

I'm sure that many times they feel like I did with the golf pro. Trying to figure out if we shared anything in common, could communicate with each other, and quite possibly, wondering why the hell am I here? Good dates that grow into good relationships rely on a myriad of factors; communication being the single most important in my humble opinion. Chemistry is great, and I think some people have a special magnetism which people and animals respond to. But for us ordinary people, communication is the key to the kingdom. We're kinda mediocre with it amongst ourselves, and we supposedly speak the same language. Although this does remind me of when my mother-in-law gave me the book *Men are from Mars, Women are from Venus* early on in my marriage. I should have taken that as a sign, coming from the mothership, but I think at the time I flipped through it and thought, hogwash. She wasn't wrong.

In love, and with horses, a lot of kindness, a lot of understanding, a lot of fun, and a LOT of listening will help you build the relationship of your dreams. No matter what planet you're from.

Chapter Twenty-Six

I Choose You

What value is yes, if no is not an option?
Leslie Desmond

Each horse comes into our lives with the chance for a new beginning. For both of us. There's a fresh new landscape to stand on together; brand new adventures to explore. It also can feel a little intimidating if we're still holding onto stories we tell ourselves, old baggage that no longer serves either of us well. When I got my gelding Skeeter as a two-year old, it was me who scribbled all over his fresh slate, good and bad. Looking back, I feel sorry for the horses that came before some of my lightbulb moments; but we only know what we know until we seek out better knowing, right?

Sometimes I wish I was much further along; with more aha! moments than scratching my head what the heck moments. More hours spent in the saddle rather than hours caring for horses with varying degrees of physical issues. My mind likes to imagine wild gallops across our hills, but my journey's been more like the tortoise than the hare. Are you Team Tortoise too? I've learned that tortoises are underrated. So I keep plugging along, working to gather those incredible light-bulb moments that illuminate and encourage. Before bringing True home, I'd promised myself I'd focus on three key things: relationship, choice, and, being with the horse before me. They sound kinda basic when written down, but these three principles have set me on a whole new learning journey.

In the past I've focused on how to "do" things. Things like driving horses around, making them go. This time, my first priority is to focus on how True *feels* about what we're doing. Learning how to drop that urge to "drive him" or to make him move is hard because it's kinda built in. Now, rather than rely on making him move with flags or lead ropes, I have to muster up that change in my own energy. It's challenging and exciting not to rely on external tools to ask for a change in True. For our relationship to develop, I have to develop the eyes to see the signals True's giving me and the ability to let him know I heard him. Our partnership, or relationship, is a two-way street. Not, my way or the highway. Sounds like it should be simple, doesn't it? But it's a way of being with horses we can be rather careless about.

The second thing I'm working on is choice. We talk a lot about choice with people, but choice with horses? Weird, right? We're usually the ones choosing, or enacting agendas of what we want to do. Warwick Schiller and Josh Nichol—two incredible horsemen who've been around to see all the different approaches, are fired up for presenting things as choice to horses. As Josh has put it so powerfully, it's about not taking something that isn't offered. That gets me right in the heart. We do that so often; sometimes we don't even realize we're doing it. Having my horse choose what I'm offering puts the onus on me. I shouldn't call it an onus; it's an opportunity. Even something as "simple" as haltering is an exercise in choice if we choose to see it that way. Rather than chasing after True's head I ask him, "can you put your head here?" When he isn't ready, he likes to take the halter in his teeth, so I move back and wait. I offer it again and this time he says yep, let's do this.

I've been asking him to choose me at liberty. He comes running up to me if he's in a pasture alone, but add the draw of those sexy girls, Satin and Wish, and I'm WAY less compelling. It's on me to compel the socks off of him, to emanate positive energy and general awesomeness. That job's on me, and boy, is that a challenge. I also let him know that I see what he's telling me, it's give and take, and we navigate our way to come alongside one another. When he chooses me, in the pasture, with the girls, I feel like having a parade for myself. For us. Sometimes it feels so darn amazing I yell "Good boy, look at you!" True looks at me like he can hardly believe I'm his. I'm not sure if he's happy about it or still trying to figure out his weird new human.

And last, and maybe the biggest lesson for me, is to be with the horse before me. To let go of my expectations of what I thought we'd "do" and go with whatever the moment presents, with the intention of both of us coming out the other side the better for it. Oh, expectations; you're so dang sneaky. We get so focused on how we want things to be, and we can get a little thrown by that. Or a lot thrown by that. Like I was when True first arrived and all the hullabaloo started between him and the mares, and between him and Junior. In my expectations, everyone played nicely together right away. I reminded myself to work with what is. And guess what? Fast forward a few months and everyone is playing (semi) nicely with each other. Funny how things work out with a liberal dose of time and patience. Time is the great washing machine.

And as Mark Rashid always says, remember to breathe. Funny how often I forget to do just that.

Chapter Twenty-Seven
A Better Deal

Connection is a horse knowing that whatever you ask of them, they are considered. That your request will not exceed that which keeps them safe, and keeps them sane.
Gareth Mare

True and I'd been cruising around; walking the hills, crossing trees—building on things. We both felt good as I put him away. From my vantage point at the barn, I saw a group of riders heading into the hills and I could tell one of the horses was struggling. My stomach clenched as I watched a wreck slowly unfolding. The rider went one way, the horse the other. I grabbed a halter and headed out across our property, hoping I could help in the aftermath. The thrown rider was holding her hand; the atmosphere was frenetic and the horses were agitated. The horse who'd been in the accident was young, the same age as True, and he was really shaken. My heart was pulling me toward him. I offered to take a horse and was handed one of the other horses. As we walked back to their trailer, I could hear the person leading him giving him an earful, saying how bad he was. Each step I took felt filled with sadness. When I saw him again at the trailer he was covered in sweat, and shaking. One of the riders grabbed his lead and backed him up roughly, telling the group he needed to know who was the boss.

My heart sank. They'd said he was inexperienced, yet he'd been out in the great wide open. I'm not the greatest horsewoman, but even I had seen his sense of overwhelm shooting off him like a beacon. While they were making a plan to take the fallen rider to the emergency room, I went over to the horse and put my hand on his wither and said, "You're a good boy; I know you were just scared." For whatever it was worth, I wanted him to know. They finally got him loaded into the trailer, and took off. I walked home dejectedly, shaken and so very disappointed in myself. I'd let that horse down. I kept running different scenarios through my head as to what, if anything, I could or should have done. I felt I'd failed him. I still have a lot to learn, but I do know there's a better way than what we've done in the past, and that better way's the way I'm headed.

A way that helps us recognize our responsibility in the relationship.

A way that helps us understand how our horses think and react.

A way to build mutually beneficial relationships with these majestic but oh so sensitive animals.

It's so dang easy to overlook how sensitive they are.

It's not the horse's fault.

For feeling scared if we haven't helped them find peace.

For feeling over their threshold when what we're asking is too much too soon.

They are not being disrespectful.

They don't want to be scared any more than we do.

On my way home I asked myself, what kind of an advocate am I for the horse, if I do nothing with this experience? I mean no disrespect by writing anything about what I saw. It was obvious the group was passionate about horses but sadly "show the horse who's boss" is still way too prevalent. Now I look back on before I knew there was a better way and I wish I'd known differently. I owe an apology to all the horses I've run around a round pen.

Blessings to all the horsewomen and men who are shining the light on this way.

Blessings to all of you who are working diligently to be that place of peace and clarity for your horse.

Bless the horses who walk beside us.

May we keep learning so that we can be that place of peace for them.

When we've done so, I believe we can throw a leg over, knowing the likelihood of things going well is increased a thousand-fold.

For us, and our horses.

Chapter Twenty-Eight
Salty Ears

Kind words are like honey–sweet to the soul and healthy for the body.
Proverbs 16:24

Words matter.
All of them.
The internal words we use to describe ourselves. The words others use to describe us; those we use to describe others. The words we choose to make sense of situations, of the world around us. These

past two years of the pandemic have shown us how words can be used to rally, unify, create chaos or division. Words that stoke anger; words that promote peace. What a difference it can make to how we feel when we assign a particular word to situations, people, and animals. It rained last night (every time I write "rain" I want to write Hallelujah! It seems right in these water-challenged times). I put the horses in the barn because they're big babies. They look at me so longingly when the first drop plops on them only an ogre would say no. I know they like being snug and dry and I also knew this would be the last time they'd be in the barn as any hopes we had for a wet spring are pretty much over.

As I listened to the beautiful sound of water falling from the sky last night, I thought how it feels like holy water, a blessing, falling down on our thirsty landscape. I went outside to stand in it, to write it on my memory before we begin our long hot summer of pear season and fire worries. Falling asleep with the sound of rain in my ears was a beautiful thing.

This morning I knew the crew would be chomping to get out of the barn and wanting breakfast. Everyone greeted me with his or her signature whinny or snort as I entered the barn, except True. He was wet which told me that rather than stay in the inside part of his run next to his girlfriend Satin, he'd chosen to stand outside a good part of the night. Well, that's his choice, I thought, but what's with the angry ears? I had to think of what word I wanted to apply to them because frankly, the first word that came to me was Dang, he looks pissed off!

Which is no way to start the day. I shook that label from my brain and rallied to find another. What came to me was "salty." You know that feeling when your pants are just a touch too tight, your sock is kinda but not really sideways in your boot, your underwear keep going where they aren't designed to go? And yea, I'm talking to whoever created thong underwear. You should be ashamed of yourself. I hope your mother is too.

True's ears were yelling SALTY. I had no idea why, but that's nothing new, so I reframed my mindset which was grabbing on to "well he looks angry about nothing which is unnecessary and annoying...." Truth be told, I had absolutely no idea how his night was, what kind of conversations had gone on in the barn, so I also had no solid reason to attach all my suppositions to the state of his ears. One thing I have learned, and I thank Charley Snell for, and that is, as always, the small things are the big things. When Junior came to live with us he was pretty insistent that he be fed first and NOW, and would crowd anyone when it came to hay. Charley shared that in the horse's book, three times sets a pattern, so I got on that, asking Junior to maintain my space while I threw flakes. No big to-dos, but using my energy to emit space around the hay and asking him to wait until I'd moved on before he would move in. It was a beautiful thing to see, so I did the same with True when he came here.

But those ears, oh my goodness. He was hanging on to whatever thought was motivating those ears for the longest time. Harry Whitney says, "get to know the motions of good emotions, and the motions of bad emotions." A horse who isn't feeling too good about things may show overt emotions like pinned ears, swishy tail, and biting. Emotions anybody with eyeballs can see. But there are more subtle emotions of discomfort, lack of confidence, uncertainty, and pain that we can, and should, look for. True's ears were making it easy even for me to see he had some emotions going on. I told him good morning, and stepped back to see if his ears would show any change. Nothing. Something had got his tail in a twist over the course of the night and he was sticking with it. I was waiting to move him out of the barn but the salty ears were causing a delay. Hey mister, I thought, help me out here. Give me your thought and let's get past salty. It took about five minutes of back and forth; each time his ear would flick forward I'd try to let him know I saw that and appreciated it. Finally, his ears worked in tandem and they came forward with some enthusiasm.

Horsemanship is funny. It is a lifetime journey, and it's in the big things but most often, in the small things. It is so, so easy to look past things that we deem small. Salty ears? Whatever. I'm here to move you from here to there so let's just get this done. Nope, it's gotta matter. Overlooking things like crabby food behavior, salty ears, and so many other things that can add up to become big things is too easy to do and requires a constant commitment on our part. Learning to understand what those "tells" are. Whites of eyes, crinkled eyes, tight nostrils, salty ears, turning away—they all matter. Those tells tell us something.

Some days, well, lots of days, I can get pretty discouraged with my progress. I'm pretty hard on myself. I try to reframe and ask, "What can I try to move forward?" There're usually one or ten things I can think of, so I try to move forward with them. Last night when I went to move horses into the barn, True was not interested in the process I had in mind. What seemed like a simple haltering evolved into about ten minutes of him turning his head, walking away and me saying, okay, I see that you're not down with this, so let's deal with what's going on rather than what I'd expected. Haltering seems the easy part, but as I've learned more, I've realized that all the parts add up to what your relationship will look like.

Ignoring things only tells your horse that you don't see what they're telling you, or that they don't matter to you, and does not help build their confidence in you. Haltering provided an opportunity to ask True, can you be with me? And he pretty clearly said nope. The biggest challenge we've had since he came to be here is his attachment to the other horses, so I recognize how that impacts our time together. I moved off to the side and back a bit to offer again, and he came with me but still only about half way invested. I waited, moved again, asked again. It took about five minutes until he willingly offered it to me, but they were five minutes well spent. Keywords here are "willingly offered." Not taking what isn't offered. That's a powerful premise Josh Nichol shares and it's profoundly changed how I look at my horsemanship.

But this morning after his evident ear emotions, I gotta admit, I started to think, "well, he doesn't like me much" and had to put a hard STOP on how I was processing that thought. He's an expressive little dude and I remind myself, that's a good thing! I think one of the most important lessons we can work on within ourselves is taking that judgment out of what we bring with us to our time with horses.

Horses are of, and in, the moment. They have their own internal lives that impact how they feel moment by moment. If we pay attention and are diligent, we can play a role in helping them to feel good and then being with us becomes a place they feel good being in. I shook off the feeling of not being that yet to True, shook off any emotion that wanted to settle in, and listened to what he was telling me.

Chapter Twenty-Nine

Analysis Paralysis

Knowledge is power.
Ignorance is bliss.
But curiosity – even if it had killed the cat – is king.
Kim Harrison

Cats get a bad rap for being curious. Luckily for cats, they've got those nine lives working for them. Cats get into absolutely everything. If there's something new in the environment, they're the first ones to check it out, sit on it, sit *in* it, or kill it. Just last night Callie was investigating a vase of beautiful roses Pat had given me. I'd been watching her thinking, "oh, she's so darn curious and cute!" just as she knocked the vase off the counter shooting glass, water, and roses everywhere. Not cute at all; not at all. So many bad words were said. Callie had the good sense to disappear while I flopped around in the kitchen, smoke coming out of my head, mopping up five gallons of water and a million glass shards.

But, that's what we love and admire about cats, when we're not furious with them—their all-around boldness in their environment. This morning I watched Callie crawl all over Pat's new-to-him boat. She misses nothing. She checked out every part of it, from stem to actual stern. She's into everything and if there's a ladder anywhere, she's on it. I love watching her curiosity for anything she can get her paws on. Except my roses.

Humans, on the other hand, have a conflicted relationship with curiosity, and it's been that way throughout history. The saying "curiosity killed the cat" really meant mind your own beeswax and don't ask questions that don't concern you. When kids are little, they ask questions about everything and let's be honest, it's exhausting answering all those wonderful what-if why-not what's-that questions. Sometimes even the saintliest moms want to tap out and say ENOUGH. Stop talking; just get mommy a popsicle please and go to sleep already. When my son Jake was little, I'd failed to tell him not to stick utensils in electrical outlets, so he learned about the power of electricity when he was four. Curiosity, and even bigger than that, wonder, are beautiful things we can become immune to. We get settled into routines and do the same things the same way every day. Coffee is one of those things, but coffee's a sacred pursuit, so that's different.

Many of us are at a place with our horses where we feel less than. We watch the journeys others are on, and it can feel like everyone else is so much further along. I can get analysis paralysis around horses. I think we all start off natural and it's too darn bad we can't stay that way. Fear of performance, of being critiqued by others can cause us to freeze up. Too often, we fall into a fear-based mindset of "be careful, be very very careful" not to do anything wrong. Now I realize how that's held me back, and not been fair to my horses (or myself). Sometimes when it's just me and my horse, that sense of "less than" comes creeping in. You know it, that feeling where you start to doubt yourself and those doubts grow, and then snowball to the point where you're thinking it's better not to do anything, rather than "mess" something up. We can end up thinking that doing nothing is better than doing something, anything, with a degree of uncertainty.

That's where curiosity can add the extra something we need, kinda like secret sauces makes a fish taco go from bland to BAM. I watched Callie crawl over the entire boat learning it with unabashed curiosity. It's a beautiful thing to see, though for all I know, she may be scoping out the best spot to pee in it to mark it as her own. I've been there, done that, (not with Pat's boat), but with analysis paralysis. I don't want to bring that to this new relationship with True, so I've been pumping myself up to capitalize on my innate sense of curiosity and wonder. I can find wonder on a walk with my two silly dogs. In some ways I feel like Callie, buzzing with thoughts about everything around me. The beauty of the hills, even in their summer-fried brown state. The old oaks are so grizzled by time yet majestic. I can only imagine the stories they could tell; stories about endurance, resilience. I think about the wonder of photosynthesis, how plants use our carbon dioxide and in turn, give us oxygen; how flipping amazing is that? I wonder how many ground squirrels were born this year, (about 2000 from the looks of it). My list goes on and on. There is so much to see, so much to experience, so much to learn. If only we have eyes to see.

When you feel stuck in your horsemanship, consider trying to capitalize on what you *do* have working for you. We all have some kind of special super power. Dig into that tool box. Curiosity and wonder are there for the taking; they don't require fancy equipment, a clinic, or special instructions. That's what I remind myself when I'm not quite sure what to do next, what I can bring to my horses when stellar technique fails me. You know what I've found? When I approach time with my horses with a framework of curiosity, and a spirit of wonder, beautiful things happen.

There's absolutely zero downside to that. Analysis paralysis,

I'm done with you.

> *I have no special talent. I am only passionately curious.*
> *Albert Einstein*

Chapter Thirty
Fiddlin' Around
(or, The Perfect Cure for Analysis Paralysis)

The most effective way to do it is to do it.
Amelia Earhart

Step into my confessional. Don't be shy, I'll start. When I was able to have a horse of my own again, I started reading up on something called horsemanship. Growing up we did something we called "just riding," but the more I learned the more I realized these two things were not necessarily the same. Shortly after I began what soon became a journey, I realized that any time spent with my horses is a learning experience, and that usually it was me who needed the learning.

I sought out horsemen and women whose words rang wise and true. I started with John Lyons, which then led me to others, and onward to where I am today. Mr. Lyons introduced a bunch of us to this journey. I'll always remember something he'd written about how much you can tell from leading a horse, and how 15 minutes a day spent doing so could have huge value. Yawn. So boring. I wasn't interested in leading my horse around; I wanted to DO things.

Fast forward some years, slow forward others, to a Five-Day Intensive Horsemanship clinic at On the Way Ranch, with Harry Whitney. It's nerve-wracking when you're up. You may think all you need to do is lead your horse from the stall down to the round pen where the "real" stuff starts, but those eagle eyes of Harry's don't miss a thing. Silly me, I'd thought leading was the easy part. Yikes. Horse creeping up on you? Um, yep. Turns out Satin is a very polite creeper. Polite, but creepy nonetheless. Looking everywhere but where you're headed? Those laser eyes of Harry's see it all. My hands were sweaty when it was my turn to make that walk of shame, and I was wondering, "How the bleep did leading this horse get so darn complicated?"

But here's the deal. It's not complicated so much as it's telling. How things go when you're leading a horse from here to there tells a pretty good story. I hadn't realized that John Lyons was right. Leading had always been incidental to me. I grew up wanting to get from here to there and off we went. Get your horse, saddle up, and head for the hills. Literally. My friends and I ranged around the hills where we grew up, and never gave a thought to anything other than how long we could stay out until heading back before dark. This new journey was turning out to ask quite a bit more out of me. And it was pointing out things I didn't really want to look at. Eagle-eye Harry sees those little gaps and knows they're really not so little. Dang it anyway.

Which leads me to fiddlin'. After spending five days in concentrated effort (and fun, just to be clear) that long drive home gives you lots of time to think. Thank Heaven for Cheetos, they help me process. Home, where there aren't any eagle eyes, it's easy to lose sight of those "little" things. It's much easier to let things that seem like boring basics sneak off a little there, a little bit there. To let things head into the gray zone I'd been inhabiting with my horse (I told you we were going to confession—you're next). What was so perfectly clear in the clinic setting made me anticipate impending doom (or what one of Harry's clinic participants so aptly named "the great undoing") as I began to think "please don't make me have to be clear and concise when I am home ALONE." I was trying to figure out how to keep that good mojo going and the magic dust that had been sprinkled on Satin from falling off when we're back home. Until I remembered Harry had mentioned fiddlin' around, and how it could help you get things figured out. I could pull that off. I had plenty to do and plenty of space to fiddle around here. Some of that fiddlin' was working on walking. That's super anti-climactic sounding but it sure pointed some big things out for me.

When I'm at a loss or figuring things out with True, I fall back to fiddlin' and so far, it's serving me well.

Years ago I'd read what John Lyon's had said about all you could learn from the seemingly simple act of leading a horse. Now years later, Harry confirmed it. Harry told us a story about an interesting conversation he had on a flight. He and another man had to sit facing each other (long-legged guys like to sit in the bulkhead—I know because I'm married to one) and the gentleman asked Harry what he did. Harry told him, and rather than the blank looking response Harry had expected, the man lit up. Turns out he was in an education doctorate program and he was very interested in *how* Harry did what he did. "Tell me how you'd teach something very complicated?" he asked. Harry talked to him about leading a horse. The man looked at him and said, "No, teach me something complicated!" To which Harry replied, "That *is* the most complicated thing."

Chapter Thirty-One
See It, Feel It, Trust It

Now faith is the substance of things hoped for, the evidence of things not seen.
Hebrews 11.1

RecentlyPat and I watched a movie starring Robert Duvall. I love Robert Duvall. I love all things Robert Duvall. I would watch him watch paint dry, I love him that much. I also miss my grandfather dreadfully, and Pat teases me that I'm in search of an adopted grandfather. I do like to pretend Mr. Duvall would love to be my adopted grandfather, if only our paths would happen to cross.

I digress. Golf's the backdrop of the movie, and golf is just not my thing. Such a small ball, such a small stick, that small hole—it makes no sense. It seems a sport intended to drive people to drink. But my love for Mr. Duvall was enough to overcome my feelings about golf.

The story is about a young golfer, Lucas, whose life and golf game go into the toilet. His relationship with his oppressive father is, well, oppressive, and as it all implodes, he falls apart on the golf course in a gloriously public way. He soon finds himself trying to leave it all behind by hitting the road but he ends up driving into a ditch in Utopia, Texas. I felt for Lucas; we've all ended up in a ditch of some sort at some time in our lives.

Mr. Duvall (Grandpa, from here on out) becomes disenchanted Lucas's mentor. Under his gentle mentorship he helps Lucas get back to believing in himself, address the frustration and anger he feels in life (and in golf), and finally, he helps him find his way back to confidence and his love of the game. At heart, it's a story about faith, about God, and about trusting yourself. Grandpa Robert's motto is "see it, feel it, trust it." I immediately started thinking about horses, and about how many of us have lost, or are losing, our confidence over time. It happens. We worry about making mistakes; we worry about getting hurt. We worry about all kinds of things, and all that worry rolls over onto and into our horses and our relationship falters. Our cup of worry starts filling up. And though the beautiful Scripture verse from Philippians tells us, "Be anxious for nothing"…well, that can be a tough one. Worry is such an easy place to land.

So how does see it, feel it, trust it work outside of the movies? I gave that quite a bit of thought. To see it, in my mind, implies that you've done the work, or as Warwick Schiller says, you've built the foundation of basics everything else is built upon. You haven't cherry-picked parts only to leave holes and gaps behind. You've helped your horse gain trust and confidence in you and themselves. Once you've done the work, know you've done your part and "see" it happening. Imagine it, envision it, see it occurring.

And feel. The great horseman Bill Dorrance believed in feel so much he dang well titled his book "True Horsemanship through Feel." So, what is feel, and how do you feel it? Many great horsemen have tried to explain it, and some say you just have it or you don't, while others say you can develop it. Think about little kids; their curiosity, wonderment, enthusiasm, and you-know-what's-to-the-wall approach to the things they love. Until we give them reason to feel otherwise, they tend to enter into new things with all the confidence in the world that they can do it. They see, they feel, and off they go.

Somehow, as adults, we tend to mistrust our own abilities in so many ways, so many arenas. Somehow the confidence and derring-do of our childhood gets flattened out as we grow older. The childlike shine wears off of us way too fast, but imagine if we could repaint ourselves with that shine! Of course, we need to do our due diligence first—to be honest with ourselves about whether we've chosen our partners wisely. Humans, and horses. Some may be flashy and appealing, but aren't right for us. Wise partnership sets us up for building the relationship in a safe and positive way. But once we've done that, what if we put our heads away for a little bit? Get out of our heads and let the energy and the beauty of our horses permeate our being. And then, trust it. Trust that we've got what it takes. Empathy, kindness, wisdom, fun, all the good stuff.

Kids get it right about fun. Fun's a muscle, you've just gotta exercise it. Don't let other people dissuade you from using what you've got inside of you. I am so grateful people can't see some of the things I try when I'm trying to get something good going with my horses. If you read my first book, you'll know that I've been called out for having chicken wing arms. Well, I survived, and my arms are working just fine.

As I was driving home the other day I thought, if I don't believe in myself, how is my horse going to believe in me?

My goal is to be all that and a bag of chips to True. Or a bag of Cheetos.

See it, feel it, trust it. And then go. Do. It.

Chapter Thirty-Two
(If) Patience is a Virtue

Patience is the art of hoping.
Luc de Clapiers

If patience is a virtue, then I'm getting a B-.

It's really never been my strong suit. I still have a scar on my index finger from an alligator lizard bite when I was about nine. We'd been trying to catch him and had set up an elaborate trap. When the lizard was almost there, I couldn't stand it and reached down to scoop him up before he got to the trap. Spoiler alert. Alligator lizards are *very* bendy and usually pissed off.

And even today, when the dogs and I were walking, we spied a little hidey-hole in a tree trunk and more than anything I wanted to stick my arm in there to see who was hanging out inside. Wisdom prevailed but dang, it's taken me a LONG time to learn some lessons. I've always been geared for jump first, figure it out later. Having two puppies, who have now become young dogs, during this pandemic has given me ample opportunities to practice patience but I still chafe at it. BE PATIENT! I impatiently tell myself. Daily. But what is patience?

We tend to think of it as a biblical principle but it's more like a hodgepodge of all kinds of traits like self-control, humility, mercy, generosity; ways of being that help us (and those around us) during stressful times. I remember very clearly a time in my life when I felt like the circumstance I was facing was utterly hopeless because I couldn't figure it out on my own. One afternoon as I was praying, I heard God say so clearly, as if it had been written on the wall, *do you trust me?* I looked around, like God may have been asking someone else. Hmm. Busted. I plead the fifth. It took me a while, a long while, to answer that question. I'm embarrassed how long it took me. Yes, I do, I thought, for other people, but not me, not in this situation. It took me a lot of flopping around like a fish to realize His ways aren't my ways. His timing isn't my timing.

It's hard to be patient when our situation seems hopeless. We've all experienced lost dreams, crushed hopes, broken hearts. It's taken me longer than the average bear, but I've finally learned that belief and patience can see you through the valley and into the sunshine again.

That's why I love this verse from Jeremiah 29.11....

"For I know the plans I have for you,' declares the Lord, 'plans to prosper you and not to harm you, plans to give you a hope and a future."

How beautiful is that?

Chapter Thirty-Three
The Spirit of It All

Horsemanship is a way of being around a horse that fits the horse.
Ben Longwell

We humans have a very checkered history of taking and using things. Things, people, animals. Horses are too often caught in the crosshairs of our want.

Looking at them for what they can give us and extracting use from them, sometimes with a terrible lack of humanity. It makes my heart hurt to think of all the mishandling and abuse horses have suffered over the years, and still do today. We used to call it breaking horses. That oughta tell us something.

Horsemanship has challenged me physically and emotionally. There've been those intoxicating AHA! moments we love so much, and many days where even getting the basics going seems to elude me. In my search for learning, I've fallen for gadgets and regimes; been fooled by all-hat-no-cattle trainers a time or two. But over time, I've kept searching for ways of being with horses that make sense to my head and my heart. I've found my way to people who are all-in for the horse and ways of being with horses that honor the horse above the activity. I am so grateful for the horsemen and women who have shown me there is such a different way.

Tom Dorrance, one of the indisputable GOATs (Greatest Of All Times, for those of us over 50) of horsemanship said in his beautiful book *True Unity*, "As I think back through the years, I realize I've felt the horse's spirit all my life, but didn't have a name for it. I am beginning to believe it may be the most important factor—that the rider recognizes the horse's need for self-preservation in mind, body, and Spirit."

He capitalized Spirit, by no accident, and did nothing to take it away or to break it. It doesn't get better than that.

To horses.

For their generous spirits.

Their extraordinary beauty.

For the incredible grace they show us clumsy humans.

The air of Heaven is that which blows between a horse's ears. Amen to that.

Chapter Thirty-Four
Honoring the Wisdom of Years

Getting old is like climbing a mountain; you get a little out of breath, but the view is much better.
Ingrid Bergman

    Elder is such a beautiful word; old, not so much.
    Old takes away the honor, the beauty of a life many years lived. Simba was my oldest guy, but he was so much more than "an old horse." He was rescued from living on a pile of rocks with a goat for a friend. They both were starving until Angie and Ronnie rescued him. The owner was unable to care for them any longer, and was

grateful to someone for intervening. Who'd have known that Simba the rescue would in turn rescue me after I broke my back?

At first, I thought I was fighting to find my way back to who I had been before my accident, but along the way I realized I would never be that person again. I also was trying to find my way back into the saddle, and never imagined that dear old Simba would be the one to do just that. Simba had been retired for a few years when I was struggling to figure out how I'd ever ride again. And then one day, as clear as spoken words I heard...

"Ride me."

And I did.

Not once, but three times until Simba very plainly said, "ENOUGH, I'm retired; find somebody else to take it from here."

We were more than survivors together. We shared a kinship. Simba got me, and I got him. We shared many years together, became older together, and hopefully I am wiser for all the lessons I have learned since. Simba already was wise; he sure didn't need any help from me.

When our elder animals start to fail, it's on us to balance that edge of knowing when. It happened so much around here lately I felt like too many of my conversations with my aging animals this past year were, "Are you okay?"

The rest of that conversation, the unspoken part, the heart-wrenching part, goes like this:

"If and when you tell me you are not okay, I will be there for you. Every step, every moment; no daylight between you and me and the thing that needs to be done. No matter how it hurts my heart; no matter how much I don't want to make that call. No matter what, I will do right by you."

Long ago I reconciled myself to the dark side of love.

The painful, knife-bite of saying goodbye. Of loss, and grief. I hate it, but I will pay that price any day for the light side of loving animals.

With gratitude for the joy, the unwarranted love, the way my heart swells in the company of animals.

The way they somehow lead me, lead us, to be our better

selves.

So each morning of this past year, I would hold my breath as I walked to the barn, not breathing until I'd counted heads, then sigh a sigh of relief when everyone was up and waiting for breakfast.

A quiet sigh, grateful to have one more beautiful day together. And then one evening, I knew that Simba would not be waiting for breakfast in the morning. I can still feel the searing pain of that realization, that the day I'd been dreading was here. It's hard to do what has to be done, and that will never change.

He's been gone months now, but some days I feel like I can still see him. When the sunlight pouring through the trees catches in the spaces between the leaves it reminds me of his golden glow. On cold crisp mornings I can still see Simba's old man mustache glistening with frost caught on his whiskers. I can still see the puff-like dragon's breath warm the chill air around his beautiful wise face. In the days before losing him I tried to memorize everything about him, and emblazon those images on my heart so I would never forget it. I miss him every day. It doesn't really go away, does it?

I have not forgotten any of him.

He was a funny elder. I think he had what I took to calling old-timer-itis. Some days he'd happily sit on my lap if he could. Other days, especially days with static electricity in the air, I was the devil incarnate and he'd dodge away from me as I'd climb through the fence to say good morning.

It's okay.

Chapter Thirty-Five
Inside Out

I'm old enough and cranky enough now that if someone tried to tell me what to do, I'd tell them where to put it.
Dolly Parton

One of my dreams is to swim with sharks. Half of you are saying, "Me too!" and the other half are saying, "Why, you're as mad as the Mad Hatter!" But, it's not surprising because the world is also divided into people who love pumpkin spice lattes and those who don't. Don't even get me started on how divisive nutcrackers are. Pat and I'd taken a short trip to Mexico and it coincided with hammerhead shark season. I've been talking about swimming with sharks for years, and this time, we did it. We signed up to do just that. I was excited/terrified, just like you are after you decide to do something you're so excited about, but on the other hand, it terrifies you, too. Sleep was hard to come by that night but morning finally came and we headed into town. We were walking down the marina on our way to the boat when a lovely young cosmetics hawker called, "Hey, lady, try this eye cream; let me show you how it can help you!" I smiled and laughed and said, "Thanks but no thanks, I need more than eye cream." And she said, "Oh yes, you do."

Well, okay then. That's a fine way to sell products, not. I smiled back at her, shaking my head and laughing as I thought, beautiful young woman, you have no idea. Dark circles? Truly the least of my concerns. And, you were probably thinking I'd combed my hair with a stick this morning because that was just about right. I'd been wearing a hat because I needed a haircut desperately but that's what rubber bands and hats are for. I don't really care about my dark circles or my hair right now. I was on a fulfilling-a-dream mission; walking down that marina, eyes sparkling as I was getting ready to step into my dream. Ready to go out onto the ocean in search of one of the earth's most beautiful creatures; to slip overboard, and beneath the surface of the water, into the realm of the shark and to live a dream. She accepted my disinterest and looked for the next baggy eyed woman to walk by.

Some dreams are just too slippery to hold on to. Just as we were about to slip into the water, something broke on the boat, and we had to limp back to shore. It was pathetic. Turned out this dream was a dream deferred. Hot tears welled up uncontrollably in my eyes. It reminded me of how it felt to be a kid again, running full tilt on the playground, only to trip and hit the pavement. My disappointment was dripping off my face, but I was proud of myself for stepping out of my comfort zone, and to know I'd tried. Pat took my hand and guided me to a nearby margarita and promised me that some other crazy day, we'd try this again.

Adios Mexico. The next day we were back into our real not-swimming-with-sharks-lives like we were never gone. The dogs were so ecstatic to see us Maisy almost knocked my teeth out. I've always wondered how time feels to dogs; did the three nights we were gone feel like three months or three minutes to them? Do they feel how fast it goes or are they so utterly in each moment that the passing of it has little import to them? Wouldn't you like to know what dogs think? Whatever it was, they were so excited to see us I almost needed a tooth implant.

As I unpacked, I found that little sample of eye cream the young hawker had given me. That little promise of beauty. If beauty is in the eye of the beholder, why are we bombarded by media telling us we need help fixing our outsides? And why do we fall for it? Buy the stuff, and bam, you'll be beautiful. Beauty *is* lovely to behold, but the things I've found to endure are those things that come from the inside, what we exude out to the world. All those things we've fought hard to learn, to become. Things like kindness, and passion; of resilience carved out of trials thanks to healthy doses of laughter and the gift of true friendship. That little sample made me think about friends who've ridden through many a wet saddle blanket to get to this point in our lives resilient and grateful. We've felt the joy of dreams that came true, the pain of those that died, and the disillusionment of those that were never given a chance. All the things we've held in our hands and all the things that have fallen through. The tears we've cried, the nights spent on our knees praying, broken marriages, all the losses: lost pregnancies, lost parents, lost friends, and the should never be experienced loss of children. We've experienced so much it's no wonder our faces show it. I thought about that beautiful young woman again and all she'd learn as her own years flew by. I knew she didn't see it, but we used to shine like diamonds just like her. We used to live in our youth just like she was, and now we live from our hearts, and it's all good.

It is all for the good.

We've learned the lessons time's ruthless passage teaches. That beauty is in the eye of the beholder, and if we're lucky, our eyes learn how to see what matters. We've learned that it's what shines out of our eyes, and what a welcoming place your heart has become, no matter what this world has thrown you. Our hearts have been broken, been mended, grown expansive, and most of all, our hearts have stayed the course. I feel so blessed by sharing this journey of life with friends whose beauty radiates off of them from the inside out. Who keep on smiling, keep on trying. I love watching them expand their horizons, watching them shake off their fears and set off in search of discovery. I am proud to cheer them on.

So here's to all of us who could use a little eye cream. Or more.

Here's to the sweetness of friendship, of laughter bubbling up from our souls, and the beauty of horses, sunshine, and hot coffee.

I hope you let your light shine full force today.

Heaven knows the world needs it.

Chapter Thirty-Six
Is the Horse Water Still On?

Not to brag or anything, but I can forget what I'm doing while I'm doing it.
Anonymous

    I felt like somebody, somewhere, would appreciate this reminder.
    You're welcome.

Chapter Thirty-Seven
Bit by Bit

We're all looking for the end result all the time, we want our horse to do this and this, but we don't think about rewarding him when he gets ready to do this and this. A horse is right here right now, trying to get through the day. How many of us are?
Joe Wolter

Spend any time around horses and horse people, and you find that we've all experienced different degrees of, Oh, You're afraid? Well, cowgirl up already. Something feels off? Well, don't be a baby, just get on that horse. It's kind of madness really, when you think about the fact that horseback riding is more dangerous than skiing or motorcycle riding. This is coming from me, a mother who said, Oh hell no! any time my sons brought up riding motorcycles. This from a woman with one broken back and five horses. I'm slapping myself upside my head right now for my own inconsistencies. When we ride horses, we're atop a survival-based animal with thoughts and feelings of its own. Unlike motorcycles. A healthy appreciation of that isn't a bad thing. It's a smart thing. It's something I learned pretty late in the game, and go figure, just about like everything else I do, I learned it the hard way. I tell my sons, listen to your Dad, not me, I just about always did things the wrong way first. My accident put things into a new perspective for me. I got hurt badly, and though I wanted to ride again more than anything, that desire came coupled to a newfound fear of doing just that.

Not too long ago a friend was talking to me about her new horse and admitted that she had a lot of apprehension about throwing a leg over. It's not uncommon; there's a lot of "ignore how you're feeling and soldier on" approach with horses. I sure appreciate honest discussions about fear. Fear. Apprehension. Worry. Sound familiar? Fortunately, I'm not afraid of anything. Ha. I've heard that from so many people who've also experienced accidents and are trying to find their way back into the saddle. It can be a lonely place, thinking you're the only one who feels that fear. I'm not sure there's comfort in knowing you're not alone, but you are not. Our horses have fear too. Sometimes lots of it. They've come from different places, different experiences, but many times they share the same basic story. They've been handled by people with good intentions, mostly, but with a focus on "doing" more than how your horse is *feeling* about the doing. We're a mixed bag of skill sets and attitudes and horses have to navigate the crap shoot we throw at them.

Fear can cripple us or it can teach us. Our quiet inner voices are telling us things we need to hear, but they often get overshadowed by those external voices telling us to buck up. We've gotten so used to shoving down our own instincts, but who knows you better than you do? If we're afraid to throw a leg over, what if we gave ourselves permission to wait until that feeling changes? Sitting in a saddle is the cherry on top, for sure, but so much good work can happen in a million other ways, too. EVERY interaction we have with our horses says something to them; conveys our intent, the state of our heart to our horses. There's so much we can do to help them, and they in turn can help us.

We *can* move our horsemanship forward *and* help our horses feel good about it in so many small but meaningful ways before we ever sit in the saddle.

If fear has thrown you for a loop, please know you're not alone. Friend, I see you. I've been there. If fear grabs at you when you think of throwing a leg over, listen to that. Please don't let shame shove you into taking a step you're not ready for. It's okay to take your time. Not everyone's Ray Hunt. Remember that it's not only us that may not be ready to ride yet; many horses also have physical and behavioral issues that need tending to before they are ready themselves.

Small things matter to our horses and they're right before us, when we open our eyes and our hearts to feel for them. And they're things we can do even when we're afraid. Especially then. We can… acknowledge that ear flick. That ask for space. The frozen I'm somewhere else stare. Work on leading so it becomes so fluid and seamless that a small child could lead your horse. Focus on their thought, over their feet. These are the "small" things I focused on until I felt confident I was ready to get back in the saddle. The things I focused on bit by bit, until one day I knew I was ready.

When your horse believes that you see what they're expressing to you, that their voice is being heard, well, then the magic can happen. Sometimes it just happens bit by bit. And that's okay. It's still magic. It's all part of the journey, and sometimes we just need to stop and stretch our legs to get the kinks out. Fear and worry sound awful and they are, when we're in the midst of them. It's an experience you and your horse may be sharing, but it's not forever. It's just right now, talking to you. Envision the (near) future where you're both breathing deeply, eyes clear and soft, your ponytail and your pony's tail are swinging easily, looking joyfully out toward the horizon.

Then, swing up into that saddle and ride out.

Chapter Thirty-Eight
Lessons from a Waitress

To serve is beautiful, but only if it is done with joy and a whole heart.
Pearl S. Buck

Do you remember the book *All I Really Need to Know I Learned in Kindergarten*?

It made sense. Be kind to others, keep your hands on your own stuff, take a nap when you're tired. Eat healthy snacks throughout the day so you don't get hangry. Stuff like that. There are lots of days I wish someone would give me a graham cracker and a tiny little cup of apple juice and make me take a nap.

Years ago, I went up to the mountains to get a free ski pass and I stumbled into a job as a waitress. The first job I got was working in the kitchen, chopping piles of potatoes the size of Mt. Everest. When they realized I was a danger to myself and the whole kitchen, I was moved to the restaurant. I was thrilled (no more danger of thumb removal) but clueless. I'd never waitressed before and fortunately the woman I worked with was a consummate professional. She was only a few years older than me but she'd done it for years and she was crazy good. Her diplomatic skills were Kissinger-level. Nothing threw her. She could handle the entire restaurant by herself, so I tagged along and tried to learn all I could from watching her.

Someone had the great idea to place the cooking area at the front of the restaurant where everyone could see the process. Unfortunately, the cook was a madman and if anything went wrong, he would bang pots and pans LOUDLY to express his displeasure. The menu plainly stated they had a No Substitutions rule, but you just couldn't stop people from trying. Denver omelet minus the ham, cheese, and bell peppers? No problem, right? I cringed anytime someone tested the rule as we'd have to take the order up and wait for the explosion. It was impressive. Pots, pans clanging and banging, eggs thrown here and there, but she didn't flinch. She'd wait patiently until he calmed down and started to fill the order. She'd go back to her table, refill hot coffee all around, complimentary juices here or there, and sometimes, when the explosion was extraordinarily grand, mimosas for the table. She'd made waitressing an art form. I've never forgotten her. I hope you are well and have had a kick-a$$ life Annette, you deserve it. I learned so much from that job and formed life skills I use every single day.

Recently we took a quick trip to the mountains and ate breakfast at a cute local cafe. That little place was a lesson in how to do everything right. It could have been run by the waitress who trained me, it was so on point. Friendly people, excellent food, excellent service.

Everything with a smile. And it reminded me all over again of the lessons I learned as a waitress.

Smile when you greet people.
Ask them how their day is.

Be prompt, be courteous, and when things go sideways in the kitchen/life/horsemanship don't avoid your table/problem/horse and hide. Face it head on.

Make sure their glasses are filled, their coffee is hot, their drinks spot on.

Make sure that whatever you're selling or presenting is the best that it can be and stand behind it with a smile.

We make life very complicated. Horsemanship and life can both benefit from slowing it down, simplifying. Sometimes it really does just come down to a genuine smile and asking someone how they are. Horses and humans.

And oh yea, a bottomless cup of coffee or a horse cookie never hurts.

Chapter Thirty-Nine
What's the Definition of Insanity?

*If we keep doing what we're doing, we're going to
keep getting what we're getting.*
Stephen Covey

    Doing the same thing the same way over and over and expecting to get different results? Yep, that's the one. Guilty as charged. I walked down to the barn to move Sundance and found him standing at the gate as if he can't get past it, even though to his left there's no fence to stop him. We've been moving fences around and left the gate standing but it's like the gate to nowhere, with wide open spaces to the left of it. But just about every morning he waits by that gate for me to open it and move him. Just this morning I was thinking, hey you big dope there's no fence on one side of the gate and feeling rather amused about his failure to adapt...until I walked back up to the house and saw one of our short little yard lights was broken—again. I keep putting it in that spot because I want it in that spot, and every time Pat backs his boat up he knocks it over. So rather than move the light to a different spot I just buy a new light. I'm on my third light.

Doing the same thing the same way over and over and expecting to get different results? Guilty as charged. This morning I looked at it and laughed and thought here I am poking fun at Sundance for standing at the gate when he could just head left around it, and yet here I am, sticking that stupid light back in the same spot that is just not working. Oh so guilty.

I was thinking about how sometimes we just get stuck on how we approach things with our horses and how we think things have to be done even though the results aren't the best. Lack of clarity, lack of consistency, lack of confidence; getting stuck on a hamster wheel of diminishing returns for both of us.

True just turned six, and every day we find that there are a lot of things he knows and a lot of things he doesn't know. Yet. Last night we were working on trailer loading and he is more unsure than I had thought he would be.

He had a little bit of an uncertain moment and it jangled both of us. My first thought was, oh crap now what? Breathe. That's always a good move. I started breathing, he started breathing, we started breathing together and walked more or less calmly out of the trailer. I knew I didn't want to leave things on that jumbled up feeling for either of us so I mixed it up and threw in a few different things he could answer "yes" to into our tries, and in and out he went. True's still not rock solid but neither am I. Every day I remind myself to check my expectations at the door; and if something's not working, then change it up. The lesson of the gate and the light reminded me that if what we're doing isn't working, stop doing it already! We are doing this together, step by step, day by day. When we hit a snag, we'll look for a different way to move forward.

    I don't know if Sundance will keep standing at the useless gate but I do know that I am going to move that damn light.

Chapter Forty
What Happened, Before What Happened Happened

Things don't go hugely wrong until they go slightly wrong.
Warwick Schiller

You've probably heard the saying "what happened before what happened happened" a time or a thousand. For me, it goes into the same category as "it depends," that is also too annoyingly true. Things don't happen in a vacuum, and if something goes south, well, there's a strong possibility there were signs preceding it. Not only were there signs, but they were flashing neon the day my ride with Wish went south. It wasn't the rabbit that precipitated my wreck, it was losing Wish's thought way before that. And even at the time it was happening, I knew I'd lost it, but I ignored that and took what she gave me. The rabbit only served as the agent for the perfect storm.

It's painfully easy (and so annoying) to armchair quarterback, and we all know that hindsight, well, we've all got perfect vision then. But, it was excruciatingly easy to unravel what happened with Wish, me, and the rabbit. Wish had become distracted and disturbed by some new things in the environment, and rather than take her at her word, I took the speed she gave me, and the rabbit only provided the final ingredient for a wreck. Icing on the crash cake. One of the most pivotal things I've learned over the years since my accident is the importance of having the horse's thought. I came from the school of "get to the feet" to get to the horse as a basic tenet of horsemanship. Well, horses don't have any problem moving their feet with their minds three miles outside the pen. But having their thought, having them with you rather than going through the motions, has been a game-changer.

Warwick Schiller tells a story he calls The Thirteen Rabbits. A rider had shared with him that her horse wasn't very smart; they'd been out on a ride and when a rabbit popped out, her horse just kept on going. Along the way another, and another, and another rabbit popped out without her horse seeming to mind too much. But when the thirteenth rabbit popped out, things hit the fan. He uses this illustration to show that when each "rabbit" (or worrisome occurrence) gets to our horse's unique worry threshold, well, hold on. Harry Whitney tells his own story of a horse walking by a rock for umpteen times with no issues until one day the horse spooks at the rock. He illustrates this with his story of a storm. It's a dark, stormy night and you're home alone when you hear a loud thump. One scary thing after another happens, loud noises, a scary phone call, thunder claps, setting your nerves pretty well on edge. You decide to hide in your room, only to smack into a table in the dark and scream and jump, terrified. Are you terrified of the table? Nope. The anxiety was there before, piling up from all the other things causing your nerves to ping.

It took a while for me to come across this approach to horsemanship. It just makes so much sense once you see what a difference it makes. I was talking with Tom Moates the other day, and he said, "Isn't losing the horse's thought always what starts things going south?" I'd bet my boot collection on it (and it's a good one). Our job, should we choose to accept it, is to deal with that first rabbit, the first scary sound, the first indication that something's creating worry for our horses. It serves neither our horse nor us well to brush it off or think, "well, that's silly, no need to be afraid of that thing." I've learned much over the years since my wreck, and having my horse's thought with me has been the overarching framework, the foundation, I've built on since. The beautiful thing is, that once your horse knows that you care about that, it builds trust into your relationship. And a relationship where you know you can count on each other is a beautiful thing. The part I love most is that you don't have to be the most skilled horse person to benefit from it. I'm not the most skilled, but I am trying to be the best observer I can be. That's a skill we all can cultivate and build upon. In horsemanship, and in life.

I'm striving to be a person who sees the things that matter.

Chapter Forty-One
Hooked on a Feeling

*This is about trust, and if you trust yourself enough to trust your horse.
That is the question.*
Nahshon Cook

  We had taken a two-day fast and furious trip to Montana for a wedding. It rained while we were gone. Real rain, not the kinda sorta kind, but rain that registers on our ever-hopeful rain gauge. The horses were thrown a bit, as rain in September in this poor desiccated state is a rarity. We got back late after frustrating flight delays. I headed out with my headlamp to say hello to the horses who were milling around looking at me like, "Why are we wet? What is this stuff?" They were muddy and a little disheveled but okay. I couldn't wait till the next day to spend time with True.

Next morning, I grabbed the four-wheeler and headed to the barn, excited to see him. He's separated for meals, because he's a little, well, chubby. Sorry buddy, but it's true. Some horses do an excellent job of picking up any extra pound they possibly can and True's one of them. I got his halter and tucked under the fence, happy to be with him. He came right up to say hi but he was harrumphy; not the happy reunion I'd envisioned. He had plenty to tell me. I went to halter him and he stepped back. I stopped. I stepped off. He turned around and showed me his impressive butt. Hmm. I moved off a bit and he turned to face me but still harrumphy. I've been trying to communicate without all the usual jabbering I do, trying to emote those feelings and thoughts into the space between us so that he could feel me rather than hear me. If True were someone I was trying to impress, I'd be in trouble. Don't you hate it when you can practically hear the sound of your hopes plopping on the ground? What was so clear to me was that this was one of those times where humans make a choice.

Choice A: Well, my plan was to spend time with you doing A, B, D, and F. So put your head in the stupid halter already and let's get on with it.

Or (here's where you get to decide to put the agenda down and leave it there).

Choice B: Okay, I hear you.

Oh, shoot; this was a defining moment. We could wrestle, or I could step into what he was telling me and work with the horse before me. As emotions of disappointment rose up, I gave myself a time-out and went to the barn to clean-up. Now that I'm focusing on paying attention to how emotions (and the stories we create around them) well up, I can see patterns of how they can take over. I took a breath, let all my what ifs and whys go, and returned to it is what it is. Maybe True doesn't like orange halters? Maybe the weird weather had jacked him up? Maybe the three-day gap I was gone had meant something? I don't know and I don't need to know. True was telling me all I needed to know; his NO loud was loud and clear.

After a while of listening, asking, waiting, he came up alongside me and very nicely put his cute little head in his halter. We went out to join the other horses. We did none of the things I'd "seen" us doing, but it felt like we "did" a lot. This time around how he feels about things, not what we do, is most important to me. I'm hopeful that what we did "do" spoke loudly to True.

We allow horses to have confidence
when we don't pressure them
into something they're not ready for.
Instead of force
we let them explore it,
and we let them experience it,
and we let them ask questions of it,
and we give them time.

From **Being with Horses** *by Nahshon Cook*

Chapter Forty-Two
The Strong Silent Type

I was quiet, but I was not blind.
Jane Austen

    I feel for stoic horses. They're often described as "bomb proof, husband horse, and kids' horse." Sometimes what's overlooked in a "been there, done that" or a horse described as quiet and calm is a horse that's gone deep down within themselves as a mode of protection. Quiet horses have their own thoughts and things to say, too, but they speak softly and sometimes we just don't have the ears to listen.

Stoic horses remind me of human introverts. Just because they're not telling the world how they feel every second, they can be misunderstood. Human introverts can get a bad rap, too. Not everyone wants to talk to strangers (horses and people), not everyone feels comfortable in new surroundings or situations (horses and people), and not everyone has the same energy level (yeah, I'll say it again—horses and people).

I'm going to tell you an unbelievable story. Many years ago, a BLM auction came to our town and Pat wanted to adopt a yearling mustang. Here's the unbelievable part—I actually told him no. I had two horses at the time, Lickity Split and Skeeter. Lick was a retired rope horse, a real been there, done that kind of guy. Skeeter was a two-year old and I was busy finding ways to mess him up, unfortunately. These two guys were at opposite ends of the spectrum and I knew enough to know I'd be way over my head in the horse-starting department if we added a yearling mustang to the mix. Pat recalls this story a bit differently, but I swear he's wrong. It's such a rarity for me to say no to an animal, any animal, so I know I'm the one remembering it clearly.

But off we went to the auction, which was sad in more ways than I can say. There was one little bay stud who got our attention, and before I knew it, we'd paid a measly $150 to adopt this poor little guy and home he came with us. Holy crap. I'll never forget setting up panels on either side of the trailer to unload him, and unload him we did. Now what? The three of us stood there looking at each other. I don't know which of the three of us was more scared.

We named the little guy Luke. Luke means "light giving" in Greek. We needed all the light we could get to go from Lick, to Skeeter, and now, a yearling who'd endured more in his short lifetime than any of us can likely imagine. Fast forward again to Luke a year later and it became evident that learning went both ways. I learned as much as he did (probably more) and eventually the first saddling and first ride were under our belts. No dust, no drama, and off we went. Not too long after Luke was moving along quite nicely, it seemed we had this once-wild horse thing going strong.

Until the day Luke was asked to move into a nice little trot and he quite politely said, "No thank you." It's very obvious in the super power of hindsight that his "no thank you" was very clear, but we saw him as the nice quiet horse that just needed a little nudge. The nudge was nothing more than a little squeeze and suggestion, but a nudge was not what he needed. And not what he'd asked for.

Turned out, that nice stoic little horse had a buck like a rocket launcher and that day goes down in infamy as the day we paid new attention to what that quiet little horse had to say. Luke didn't have an angry bone in his big drafty body, but he had his own thoughts and own things to say that we'd overlooked in his quiet presentation. He told us how he felt, but he was so darn polite about it we didn't believe him and asked for more. I've always felt bad about that, and I've never forgotten it.

I've learned. Listen. Especially to the quiet ones. It's well worth the effort. Just because they're quiet doesn't mean they aren't part of the conversation.

I dedicated *Broken, Tales of a Titanium Cowgirl* to "my mustang Luke, who taught us that you should always listen to your horse, even if it takes you a long time to figure that out."

To Luke, and all those stoic horses out there. May we have the eyes to see and the ears to hear all you are telling us.

Chapter Forty-Three
May I have your Attention Please, Please!

My fashion philosophy is, if you're not covered in dog hair, your life is empty.
Elaine Boosler

   Come into my confessional and I will tell you why I do not love puppies, if you promise to keep this on the DL. When I was a teenager, my parents nickname for me was The Enforcer. It was said with love, at least that's how I'm remembering it. I came into the world loving dogs and have never been without one for long. My expectations were high and I expected my dogs to be well-behaved. Even people who don't like dogs appreciate a well-behaved dog because there's nothing fun about having a strange dog fixated on attaching themselves to your leg. Consequently, I've spent hours at dog school with every dog who's blessed my life. Cassidy the Catahoula was so insulted I'd taken her to school and kept giving me disdainful looks. She was so smart she could have taught the instructor a thing or two. Sage, our black lab, would lose her mind for treats, and writhe on the floor in a disturbing way. Scout went to dog school especially for little dogs with his also-little sister Bernice. He excelled, of course. Terriers are nobody's fools.

CJ, Georgia Rae, Kai, and all the dogs who have blessed my life have excelled at obedience. Boy, was I about to have my bubble burst. All those lovely, well-mannered dogs had given me some overinflated idea that it was actually me who was contributing in a positive way to their good behavior. Well, that bubble's burst. Maisy and Rufus may push me over the edge. Each morning as I walk these two juvenile delinquents I think about horses and asking for your horse's thought. That's always seemed so challenging to me, and yet, compared to the ping pong brains of these two youngsters, it looks like a child's play in comparison. Asking for their thought when they're thinking Squirrel! is as frustrating as filing your taxes.

Most days I've broken my no-swearing before noon rule before nine, usually after I've untangled them six times yet somehow, they're still wrapped around my legs, one going forward and one going backwards, so my arms are splayed out like Don Quixote's windmills. Their new thing is to pick up sticks. You have no idea how many sticks there are in the world. Sticks are so stupid and I tell them so, which makes them pick up more sticks. Five minutes of this and I feel like stapling my forehead to a floor somewhere dark and quiet. Asking for a horse's thought to be with you seems easy-peazy by comparison as I find myself begging, begging for the attention of these wild things. When we get back to the house, I look at the disheveled wreck of myself and wonder what the beep was I thinking getting two (not one, TWO) puppies in a pandemic. I'm pathetic.

Separately, these two are amazing. But two young dogs who

feed off each other, well, it's a you know what show. There's zero future for me in Roman Riding. Plus, I'm about 95% convinced Rufus has gamed the positive reinforcement program. He'll do something like find a huge piece of horse poop and look at me for the command "leave it" or "drop it" which he does happily and gets a treat, then picks up another piece essentially working me like a human Pez dispenser. When we're finally picking up speed, one will throw on the brakes, so I tumble over them into a heap. Maisy loses her mind around Rufus, which makes treat rewards a challenge as I'd literally need a Yeti full of rib eyes to entice her away. Bless her heart (snarky font), it's a good thing she's so dang cute. So maybe, someday, please I pray, please Lord, I would love to have their attention, before I lose the rest of my marbles. I swear it would help my no-swearing effort greatly.

Chapter Forty-Four
The Wave

If you have good thoughts, they will shine out of your face.
Roald Dahl

My best friend of forever lives a few hours away from me. We trade off visiting each other every few months. It's a blessing and a sanity saver, for us and our husbands. Whenever we're together we talk non-stop and use up all our pent-up words (for which they should be eternally grateful). Sometimes her husband asks her what we've found to talk about for the past forty-five years, to which she answers, "Oh, world peace, our kids, shoes, how toes can be so weird, what we would do if we were in charge of everything, and oh, look a chicken!" He just shakes his head.

It's a 24-hour dash of a trip, but we make the most of it. When she visits me, we do something called playing horses, walk a lot, and talk non-stop. I make her the world's best Lemon Drop (a skill I developed during the pandemic) and confirm that she's still the world's biggest lightweight. When I visit her, we talk non-stop and she takes me to Anthropologie, the happiest place in the world, where I head right to the sale corner. Last time we went shopping, I came home with a framed picture of a donkey holding a chicken on its nose. I loved it; she said I needed it, and she was right. Pat just shook his head, and hung it up in the guest bathroom for me.

On my way to her house, it's all country roads until I hit the highway. You know that you drive differently in the country than in the city. My son lives in LA where it takes twenty-minutes to drive two miles and everybody tries to avoid eye contact. But country road driving involves lots of eye contact and something called The Wave. When you drive country roads you get to dust your wave off and I was back in the groove, waving to just about every truck that passed. Have you ever noticed that about 98% of farmers and ranchers drive white pickups? Pat included.

I miss The Wave. Up where my folks live in southeastern Oregon, usually the only people you'd pass on the road were your neighbors. Each neighbor would wave, and each wave was unique. There was the stoic, keep your hand on the wheel but raise your fingers wavers (usually the men), and there were enthusiastic wavers like Nancy who just about waved her hand off her arm with her "howdy neighbor!" version.

We live in the country but my wave's become weak from lack of practice. There's a park out by our place and it'd be easy to wave to bunches of strangers which would be kind of weird, so I'm erring on the side of restraint rather than enthusiastically waving strangers down. Hence, my wave's on the down low these days. Pat shoots trap occasionally and all the older gents who are able to shoot regularly out our way tell him that they wave to me if they pass me on their way to the range, but I just keep on driving. Disclaimer: I would

LOVE to wave to you, but my odds of it actually being the right person are about 50:50 and I'm just not ready to double down on that one. I miss the wave where you didn't wonder who you might be waving at, and you just waved the heck out of them. My wave is a left hand back and forth, hand all the way off the wheel. Even if you don't use one every day you should have The Wave in your life tool box.

Chapter Forty-Five
Connection or Control?

What's coming will come, and we'll meet it when it does.
Hagrid, in Harry Potter

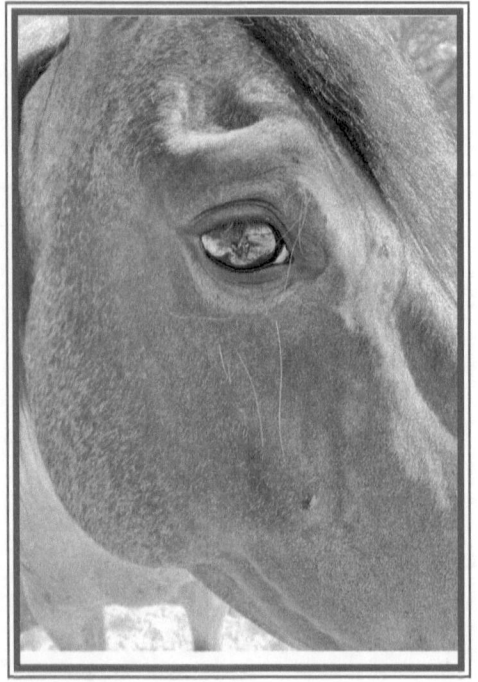

True's not a huge fan of fly spray; but let's be honest, who is? Getting your horse used to fly spray is almost always a question at clinics. It seems kinda silly, right? Why is fly spray a big deal? But fly spray, like trailer loading, and so many things our horses balk at, really isn't about the spray at all but about trust; your horse's belief in you; their connection with you.

We're most comfortable having an animal on the end of a lead rope, a leash. We attach them to the other end and then we're good! Off we go, with us dictating where we want them to go, more or less. It might not always be pretty, but we feel fairly confident we're in charge. Silly humans. The truer (and scarier) test is what happens without that physical connector. No leash; no lead rope. Gulp. Will your dog or horse still be with you? Oh, hell to the no on Maisy and Rufus. It's squirrel country gone wild around here. The squirrels got real busy this winter and now they're running amok. Lately ground squirrels have taken to dropping out of trees when I'm out playing catch with Maisy. No joke, they are actually dropping from the trees. I'm still scratching my head because they're, well, *ground* squirrels for crud's sake. Aren't they supposed to be on the ground? It would be funny but for the fact Maisy loses her mind and I lose Maisy when a squirrel lands right in front of her nose. Dropping squirrels aren't the only attention-grabbers. Heck no, we've got deer, turkeys—a hundred distractions at the ready to send Maisy and Rufus off in a flash. I'm simultaneously working on this/pulling my hair about it. They have situational recall—pretty much any situation overrides their recall unless I am carrying a steak.

Connection can feel so elusive. How do we build connection with another living being? I first heard the saying "being seen, being heard, feeling felt, and getting gotten" on Warwick Schiller's Journey On podcast with Sarah Schlote, a psychotherapist who specializes in trauma therapy. It rang all the bells for me. Who doesn't want to be seen, heard, felt, and gotten? I sure do. That's what I want in my relationships. That's what I want for True and me. A relationship that goes two ways. True was in a little bit of a spot before I got him. His owner wasn't able to be around him much and the woman looking after him was great with him, but busy with many other horses, as well. I'm not sure he was asked how he felt about too many things in his "past life," and now he's more than happy to tell you what he thinks. His ears are uber expressive—and he has a telling eye. He's a master of the you've gotta be kidding me side eye, too. He makes it pretty apparent what he's thinking; even I get it most times. Or, at least, I think I get most of what he's telling me. And he was telling me he wasn't a fan of fly spray.

Flies. They're wretched. I like most living beings but flies, mosquitos and ticks, nope. And I don't feel bad about it. They're on this list I'm keeping called Questions to ask God, along with who ate the first artichoke. Each year they arrive like clockwork when the temperature warms up, and I start my annual mission to knock out the fly population. It's a full-time job involving fly traps, fly masks, fly spray, and cussing. Satin's a champ; she appreciates the relief spray brings and lets me spray her out in the field. Wish does a little dancing around and then she stands and appreciates the assist. I'm used to spraying them without haltering, so I approached True the same way. He took one squirt and said, "nope, not gonna happen." The most immediate answer seemed to be halter him and hold on, but this was an opportunity to listen to him and assure him I can hear what he's telling me. Every day I resist the urge to just blast him and every day it improves how he's feeling about it. I let him know I see him, I hear him, I get him. I'm grateful he tells me how he's feeling. I know how good it feels when someone helps me feel that same way.

Chapter Forty-Six
Creatures of Habit

We first make our habits, and then our habits make us.
John Dryden

Only took me a couple of tries to tie a knot on a right-side tie halter. Arg. True was a pretty good sport about it but I'm sure he was thinking what-the-beep woman. I was glad there was no one around to see me struggling to figure it out. What an eye opener.
We're such creatures of habit. Brush our teeth with the same hand… put our socks on in the same order…do all kinds of things the same way all the time until something forces us to change it. Usually, it's

an accident or some kind of physical limitation that forces us to expand our go-to habit. After my little right-side experiment, I realized how this must translate to True if I am heavily favoring one side of myself and, by default, him.
What if we mixed it up to keep our brains and our skills accessible and handy?

It really helps in our work with horses so that neither one of us become so dang one-sided.

Chapter Forty-Seven
Training Tools

*We are slowed down sound and light waves, a walking bundle
of frequencies tuned into the cosmos.*
Albert Einstein

We've seen so many, right? Tie-downs, martingales, whips, sticks, carrots, flags, waving that lead rope like a propeller, and that old stand-by, cussing. If your journey's been like mine, you've probably had something to do with each of those. I look back and feel shame; shame for my clumsy use of devices to extract some action from my horses, shame for the horses I've run around a round pen, flagging them so they'd "go." Shame is like a warning light on your car; there to give you a head's up, and then take action. Sometimes it's tempting to ignore the warning light and maybe stick a piece of tape over it so you can't see it, but it's really just there to help. When I feel shame about something, I realize that's my heart telling me I've gone off-course and need to make a change. Stop doing the thing causing it. Do better. And then, let it go, because shame holds us down and keeps us from shining our brightest light.

Training tools can be useful when used well; and they also can be a crutch. It's made me realize how often I've relied on a flag rather than being clear about my intent and what I'm asking. Horses must find that very confusing. Watching people ask for a change in their horse with a change in their own energy is such an inspiration. I'm working on getting my non-verbal communication stronger so that I don't have to rely on a tool to communicate with True. The times I get that right are so cool and make me think: What if we believed we are the only training tool we need? I've been trying to unwind what that looks like and how to dig deeper in myself to find it. Maybe I could duct tape my mouth closed to be quiet around my horses. Or, duct tape my hands to my side to stop how badly my hands want to reach out and touch them. Or both. Much of that feeling comes from not having confidence in myself that I can figure things out all on my own. I'm not alone in this. My friends and I often talk about getting to a place where we feel stuck. But maybe we've underestimated ourselves into a kind of stalemate? Maybe our horses are just waiting for us to believe in ourselves, and they'll be happy to believe in us too.

Chapter Forty-Eight
Be Quiet

Silence isn't empty. It's full of answers.
Unknown

Be quiet.
I mean that nicely.
The world's a noisy place.
Our thoughts bounce around like ping pong balls at a frat party.
Shhh.
Listen to your own breath until the all the noise quiets.

Now let's bring that to our horses and see what happens.

Let the silence sit there, settle in, speak its own language.

And when that Oh look a chicken! random thought pounces into your head, tell it very kindly to get lost and start again.

Heaven knows I love words but I'm pretty sure True prefers our quiet conversations.

I'm trying.

Chapter Forty-Nine
Get in the @#$% Trailer Already

It does not matter how slowly you go, as long as you do not stop.
Confucius

My friend Leslie and her beautiful palomino mustang, aka, the marvelous Mango, were coming to visit. We'd signed up for an obstacle day at a nearby equestrian center. We're off the main highway routes so when a horse friend comes to visit, it's a big deal. Leslie's the best kind of houseguest; she's easy to have around, she brings food, and wine. Score. I was super excited, and a little nervous as this would be the first off-site adventure for us. True had loaded up in the trailer when I picked him up, but I'd learned he wasn't all that confident about it. Getting a horse in a trailer is one thing; having confidence about the trailer is another.

Now, to participate in the obstacle course he needed to be at the obstacle course. And though it isn't that far away, it's a trailer-to place. The next morning as it was time to go, he went in, but he wasn't confident about it. True was letting me know he had some doubts, so I believed him. There was that flipping choice again; what I'd planned on doing, or what he was telling me. Listening to True won out. I knew it meant more to me to have him be confident about all aspects of loading than it did to get to the event. My goal is building confidence in True (and myself), not arriving at events. Leslie supported my choice in letting go of that agenda, and they loaded up and headed out. I was happy to watch and cheer them on. Mango is a rockstar at obstacles, and she was in her element. Leslie supported her in every way and it was a joy to watch them together.

We can easily overlook the amount of worry a horse has about the loading process. It's easy to lump it together into a simple thing we call "get in the @#$% trailer already!" Been there, done that. But it's not really about the trailer, right? By nature, horses are claustrophobic and jumping into a big aluminum can isn't something they'd think of on their own. Add the anxiety of humans trying to make something happen on a schedule and it can all fall apart if the foundation to get there confidently hasn't been laid down. Most importantly, I think we let our horses down.

True and I will live to do obstacles another day. In the meantime, we've deconstructed trailer loading and yep, there are still moments, but his confidence is growing each time. That's the win for me. Could I have gotten True in the trailer? Yes. Would he have been confident about it? No. I'm in this for the long haul with him. My vision is that True becomes so comfortable loading, unloading, going everywhere, that he'll be teaching trailer loading to young horses all by himself. You know what makes a huge difference too? Hanging out with the right people. People who put the horse first and support you when you do. It's not easy to say, "sorry, this isn't happening today." But Leslie's a good one. I'm blessed by her friendship and so many like-minded people I've met along the way who support me and my horses by doing what's best for both of us.

Chapter Fifty
Imagining Dragons

But it is one thing to read about dragons and another to meet them.
Ursula Le Guin

It's been so hot this summer, and last night was windy on top of it. It was wretched. I'd been waiting for the cool of the evening to spend some time with True but it never came, so I brought him out anyway. The wind was blowing his fabulous forelock about and trying to rip off my hat. I ponied True up beside me as I started the four-wheeler and he jumped a bit as we headed off. No worries I told myself, sometimes it's windy and we both have to figure that out.

The wind was doing more than blowing leaves around when we entered the pen; it was enough to keep a witch afloat on a broom. True was full of it. He flew by me bucking and jumping like a Tasmanian Devil. '¿Qué es eso? Who was this horse? How did he get all that action going on in that little package? He went whipping by me, an invitation to join in on the chaos. He was impressing himself and freaking me out a bit. I moved to the center and stood until he swung back around and wanted to come in breathing dragon breath. Work with the horse before you, work with the horse before you, I repeated silently, digging deep and hoping I had the what-for to help him. I whacked my chinks with the end of the lead rope, stood where I was, and let out a huge exhale, turned to my left and he came up alongside me giving me a look like, "Wow, what just happened?" I let out the breath I hadn't realized I was holding and we walked out a bit until the dragon wings disappeared.

It reminded me of another hot summer day not long after we'd moved here. Nobody told me that grocery shopping on the 4th of July weekend was a terrible idea. I should have known better but I'd loaded up my little son into his car seat and headed to town. By the time I'd finished shopping the store was packed with tourists and the lines were long. The line inched along sloth-like when he decided he'd been a good sport and now he was over it. By the time we finally got to the checkout line we were both red-faced. The checker and the bagger looked at me and said, "Hey, you're doing great! This is usually where parents cave and just start buying anything to make their kid stop crying. You've got this!"

I'll never forget that. I also learned not to shop on a holiday weekend around here. But the lesson which really helped me in those early days of mothering was that just because everyone around you falls apart, doesn't mean you need to join in. In his case he was tired and hungry; I'd overestimated our ability to be gone so long and underestimated the crowds. We drove home, washed off our overheated selves, got a snack, and we both took a nap.

True's the young guy here, it was dinner time, it was windy, and he wanted to be somewhere other than where we were. It was a learning experience for us both because sometimes dinner is late, sometimes it is windy, and sometimes we have to go places we don't especially want to go. I could hear the wise words of Charley Snell in my head about not tip-toeing around our horses and being okay with helping them through challenging experiences. This one was pretty low on the challenge-scale but I believe they all add up if we keep our heads and stay above the fray. The next day, True had on angel wings. No dragons to be found.

Chapter Fifty-One
The Law of the Hammer

If the only tool you have is a hammer, it is tempting to treat everything as if it were a nail.
Abraham Maslow

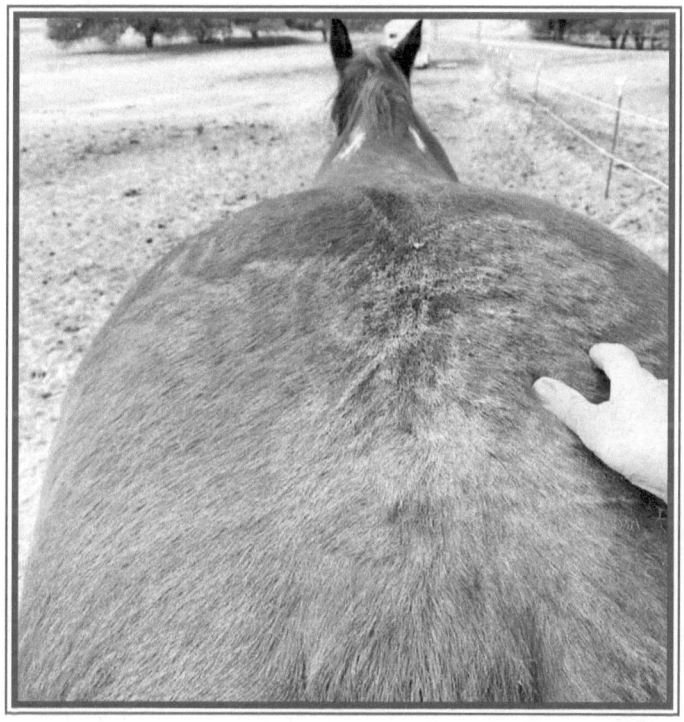

Isn't it funny how one little quote can just light up your brain?

I think this one nails it.

Chapter Fifty-Two
Why?

Ours is not to reason why, ours is but to do and die.
Alfred Lord Tennyson

Nobody wants to be known as the kid in the front row, first hand to shoot up, waving madly, signaling call on me! Call on me! Okay, that's only partly true; all the pre-med kids in Chem 194 at UC Davis did, but that's a story for another time. Just know, I was the kid in the back, trying desperately to figure out what the heck Avogadro's Number meant and why I needed to care. Now, if you were that kid, my apologies, but life has probably made you slightly less enthusiastic by now. Natural selection takes care of lots of that stuff.

Many more of us can remember hunching over our desks in a semi-hide, awkward middle-school kids afraid to draw attention to ourselves and be exposed for what we knew or didn't know. We took seats in the middle, if not the very back, eyes down so as not to catch the instructor's eye, praying we weren't called upon to answer questions. Whether you were an arm waver or an eye dropper, our relationship with questions can be complicated.

Why are we so afraid to admit we don't know everything? Read that and realize how silly it is that we even thought we could or would in the first place. The pandemic has provided ample opportunities to prove we all had much to learn. We scrabbled with each other about vaccines, no vaccines, DNA, mRNA, and masks. The science girl in me craves a survey to query how many people know what mRNA is in the first place. But we've got opinions on them all, shared loudly in the belief we had all the answers. Wrong. As we learned, and continue to learn, is that trying to keep track of what we thought we knew was like trying to run on top of a train.

When we're little guys our favorite question is Why? If you've spent any time around a two-year old you know this viscerally. They want to know EVERYTHING. Thank Heaven (and Larry Page and Sergey Brin) for inventing Google because little kids asking you why the sky is blue will send you running right there. And then modifying an appropriate reply into something that doesn't send you off talking about how blue light is scattered more than the other colors of the visible light spectrum because it travels in shorter, smaller waves usually becomes something like, "Because that's the color God made it." Google has saved so many of us from looking flat out incompetent in front of our children, only for them to find we are actually clueless when they're teenagers and we ask them what GIF stands for and to explain NFTs.

It's challenging to be questioned, and there's nothing like trying to explain something to others that sifts out what you really understand and what you're just faking your way through, which is about 50% of parenting. But that natural curiosity of kids just blows me away. I love it. They're curious about literally everything, especially things we so-called grown-ups are embarrassed by. The more potentially embarrassing, the more they want to know. And usually in public. But unless and until we get busy knocking that curiosity out of them, we could take a lesson from children. We should take a lesson from children, model their banzai no-fear approach to asking why.

Questions scare us. I was that student in college. Afraid to ask for fear I'd reveal what I didn't know. Afraid to ask an instructor who gave off such an aura of Thou shalt not ask coupled with my natural fear of asking, so many questions went unasked. I distinctly remember my first quarter, freshman year of college. That very same Chemistry class, 500 smart students, all clicking those multi-color pens, all planning on going to med school or vet school. I was so intimidated. The class was taught by a dusty old professor who'd written the text book. At the time, I would have guesstimated him to be seven or eight hundred years old. One lecture I girded myself up to ask a question, raised my trembling little hand, and bleated out the question. I can still feel the silence as the class waited with baited breath for the answer. He gathered himself out of the fugue he had been in, rotated away slowly from the board he'd been scribbling gibberish on to give me a painful glare, and said "It's in the book, I suggest you read it."

Okay. Well. That was painful. Thanks a lot Dr. Dinosaur. If I understood the book, I wouldn't have asked the question which mortified me then, and obviously, still takes up space in my brain. Years later when I had the opportunity to teach biology at our local community college, teaching was all new to me. I'd never thought of myself as an instructor, but I'm nothing if not enthusiastic, so I dove in. As I looked out from the podium across the hodgepodge of students, I realized they were all coming in with such different backgrounds. Some were advanced sixteen-year olds, doubling up on high school and college credits at the same time. Others were sixty-plus years old; they'd gathered up the gumption to go back to school to complete their degree. Others were students who hadn't done well in school, didn't like school, and struggled with the basics. A crazy quilt of students.

I thought, well, I'm new to this but I remember how I felt in school. How I'd longed for an environment where I felt safe asking questions, safe enough to say, "I don't get that" or, "could you explain it in another way?" Now, by one of those strange turns of life, I was on the other side of the podium. It felt like a tremendous responsibility, and I have always believed that. I took a deep breath, which always helps no matter what, and I told my class I believed in questions. And in fact, I said, "there may be no such thing as a stupid question." That one I had reason to doubt sometimes, but still. Sometimes a student would ask a question that was either so profound (think worm holes in deep space) and others which felt so incredibly obvious I had to take a moment. But that was my mantra, and that's how we rolled. What really mattered to me was the learning environment. Creating one that is supportive, where there's no such thing as a bad question (kinda), and where *why* is cultivated and treasured.

Kids had it right all along. Curiosity is the spice of life. Wonder, and wondering why, keeps our eyes bright and our lives interesting. Our horses appreciate being able to ask why, too. Think what a beautiful gift we can give them when we help present them with things with wonder and why at the heart of them. Why not?

Here's a lesson I've learned the hard way. Choose your teachers, your mentors, the people you look to for inspiration and information well. Putting yourself out there to learn something new, challenging yourself to grow (and especially with horses where we need to be our most open authentic selves) can be a very vulnerable place. I've seen friends quake with nerves and lose trust in their own instincts when someone they've admired or sought out tears them down or belittles them. I've been there. It doesn't feel good, but guess what? That's on them, not you. Their integrity with your horse *and* you, needs to match up with their ability. If they don't, get thee out of that round pen.

I'm trying to bring more why with my try these days. More power to us for putting ourselves out there, for trying to learn and grow. Being open to what ifs and being vulnerable with uncertainty helps us to get to the heart of what matters with horses, and our guides or teachers need to understand the responsibility they hold in their hands. We all need a safe learning environment to really be able to ask why so we can learn. Let's not settle for anything less.

> *It is not the critic who counts; not the man who points out how the strong man stumbles, or where the doer of deeds could have done them better. The credit belongs to the man who is actually in the arena, whose face is marred by dust and sweat and blood; who strives valiantly; who errs, who comes short again and again, because there is no effort without error and shortcoming; but who does actually strive to do the deeds; who knows great enthusiasms, the great devotions; who spends himself in a worthy cause; who at the best knows in the end the triumph of high achievement, and who at the worst, if he fails, at least fails while daring greatly, so that his place shall never be with those cold and timid souls who neither know victory nor defeat.*
> *Theodore Roosevelt*

Chapter Fifty-Three
The Stories We Tell

If we change the way we look at things, the things you look at change.
Dr. Wayne Dyer

It's way too easy to bring preconceived notions with us to horses. We wonder about their past lives, imagine what they experienced (it's really easy to do with rescue horses), and enter into our relationship with stories in our heads. Oftentimes those stories don't help either of us.

My first experience with Junior wasn't what I expected. His person is a friend of mine and when she wasn't able to keep him any longer, we were fortunate enough to become his new home. I'd gone to pick him up, and when I went to unload, he made a three-point turn squishing me in the corner, and blasted out of the trailer like a rocket. He's as big as a moose, and I'm not, so I became cautious about that size difference. After he'd been here a bit, I realized I was keeping a mental distance between us because those initial behaviors got stuck in my mind and colored how I approached him. It took me a while to realize that in spite of his size, he was feeling insecure and it showed up through things like that, showing his lack of confidence in a new place. And in me. Who can blame him? He'd lived with his person since he was little, and coming here was a huge change in everything he'd known, and now I was tip-toeing around him.

In *True Horsemanship Through Feel*, Bill Dorrance talks about making assumptions about a horse. I think it's especially easy with horses described as "been there, done that." Mr. Dorrance encourages us to take responsibility for a horse's worries by working on our ability to present an understandable human feel that translates to the horse. He says that when you have feel that goes both ways, you have that horse's respect and cooperation. "It's that simple." Well, I don't know about that, Mr. Dorrance. Sometimes it feels anything but simple. What Junior *was* feeling from me was distance, and it wasn't helping him at all. I decided to lean into that big moose and treat him like I wanted him to be. To let go of the stories I had in my head about him based on those first days. It was freeing. He was food dominant, and so we worked on polite expectations, thanks to great insights from Charley Snell. We slowed things down and he loads in and out of the trailer like a perfect gentleman, thanks to Charley, as well. We've formed a relationship now and it's been so fun to see his guarded personality open up. He's gone from being a big moose to being a big goofball.

The great horsewomen and men make it look pretty easy, but those of us on this journey know it's the work of a lifetime. Sometimes just letting go of the stories in our heads is the first-step to a new relationship. Stories about ourselves, as well as our horses. One of the most transformative horsemanship lessons I've (slowly) learned is work with the horse before you. Not the horse of your expectations, the horse of your imagination, not the horse in your story, but the actual one you're with, in real-time.

Chapter Fifty-Four
The Fine Art of Saying Yes

The important difference here is with win/win/win, we all win.
Me too. I win for having successfully mediated a conflict at work.
Michael Scott, The Office

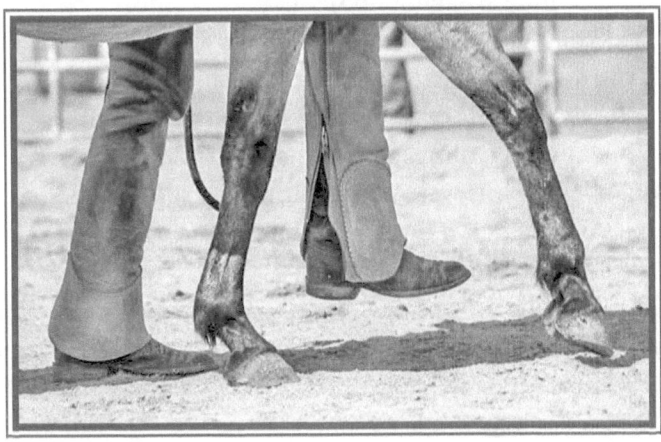

"No" is a simple little word, right? Two letters; one consonant; one vowel. Bam. No has a lock on the short word department. But simple? No, no isn't simple by any means. How does such a little bitty word carry such a heavy punch? Many cultures have multiple words for snow because it impacts their lives in so many ways. The Scots win, with 421 words for snow. Scots' language lecturer Dr. Susan Rennie wrote, "The 421 words are all sorts of things to do with snow—the way that snow moves, the types of snow, types of snowflakes, types of thaws, clothing you might wear in snow, the way that snow affects animals—we have even got a category for snow and the supernatural." I'm no etymologist but perhaps snow became so complicated because "no" is part of it?

Historically and etymologically speaking, in contrast to snow, no is defined as "not in any degree." But, just like snow, all noes aren't created equal. Which makes me think of lentils. If you asked me if I like lentils, I'd say no. I really don't. I know what you're thinking, something along the lines of "okay, but who cares?" My Mom cared a lot. Or at least it felt like she took my dislike of them just a little bit personally, and it felt like she made lentil soup way too often when I was a kid. It placed us in a table stalemate. I spent minutes of my life I'll never get back staring at a bowl of cold lentils and let me tell you, she was right. They're way better hot. I know they're good for you but I still avoid them every chance I get. But no isn't always as simple as saying no thank you to lentils. No one wants to say, "Will you marry me?" only to be met with an awkward, "Um, no thank you." Ouch. That no isn't simple at all. Things got missed big-time. It's easy to resort to Just Say No with our animals and our kids. No is easy; a default response when we've hit that hard wall of frustration. Many of us were raised with No, Don't, and Not. It's hard to extract a feel-good outcome from within a negative framework. Letting go of No takes practice!

There's a fine art to saying yes. It takes a little more work to figure out how to set things up so that you can say Yes as often as possible. Sounds kinda weird and woo woo when you first hear it, doesn't it? But setting up a Yes framework doesn't need to mean letting your kids grab all the candy at the checkout lane. We can figure out ways where Yes is the answer, and win-win-win is the outcome. I'm working hard to incorporate it with my horses, and with Maisy and Rufus. When my sons were young, I remember reading something that said if you're trying to change or shape a behavior, then it needed an opposite but positive behavior to replace it, rather than leaving a vacuum or void. My Mom was a master of it. She says I stopped napping when I was about two and had way more ideas than she needed me to have. Her go to reply to my exuberant (and unasked for) suggestions was, "Well, that's an idea!" neither telling me yes or no when she was just plain ready for me to sleep already. It was brilliant (and super annoying). We still joke about it. It's actually really fun (for me) to throw that out at her every once and a while.

Every parent who's tried to stop a child from a habit knows the struggle's real. A child who's finding comfort in their tasty little thumb likely won't stop sucking it if they are told, "No, don't do that." There're many reasons behind that self-soothing habit. "No, don't," leaves the unmet need unfulfilled and turns thumb-sucking into a thing to be ashamed of, to hide. Shame doesn't succeed in affirming anything. Maybe that little one's as entranced by the miracle of opposable thumbs as I am. Who isn't?

How do we turn the No bus around when sometimes the only word we want to yell is NO? It takes practice to let go of no, to figure out how we can we set things up for success where the answer can be yes. But. Yes. We. Can. Find. Another. Better. Way. To lean into the fine art of saying yes. I love what Warwick Schiller has done by posing "Ask yes questions" to your horse. He poses them as: questions the horse knows the answer to; questions the horse doesn't know the answer to yet but has the education to know how to search for answers and the ability to figure it out; the horse knows the answer and is capable of doing it in his current emotional state.

We've been in the habit of No for so long with horses; presenting them with no way out if they don't know the answer to the questions we're posing. And too often they don't know because we haven't presented it with clarity or helped them grow in confidence to seek out answers. We've all seen horses bear the brunt of a rider's frustration and it isn't pretty. It doesn't need to happen. We're better than that. We need to be better than that. We have resources and people who are leading the way towards a better way. It's a challenge but when you get it right, there's NO (see what I did there?) stopping you.

Chapter Fifty-Five
What if?

Tell me, what is it you plan to do with your one wild and precious life?
Mary Oliver

    What if, one day, a bright light came on.
    That light bulb in your head, and you could see yourself clearly, as you were designed. Not the stupid stuff the world tries to label you with, but something bigger.
    Much bigger.

What if you could see clearly all the mystery you are made of. Each cell, each system, each miracle of function. Of flesh, of blood, of things you can touch, and those you can only feel—like your soul, your spirit. More even.

What if you could see your place in the all of it? Combined pieces of the universe, of before, and after, of what was, and what will be. Pieces of ancient stars, space dust, and of the earth too; of loam, silt, clay.

What if the pulse of your heart mirrors the all of it? Of the oceans, of that connection with the vastness? The realization dawning that you are not just a drop in the bucket, but a part of the ocean?

What if you could feel the wonder of that, knowing you are built for a purpose, a purpose uniquely your own. And what if that knowing ignites, and begins to grow into a bright flame only you can cast, not dull and dimmed, but bright and full, filled with portent and meaning? What if nurturing that light, shining that light as only you can do, *is* your purpose? What if no matter what else happens in these days of our lives, we spend time in wonder, in spite of everything. In wonder not only of the beauty of sunsets and of what we can see, but in the realization that purpose knit every fiber of you together, the knowing that there is only one wonderful you. For you are fearfully and wonderfully made. And please don't you forget it.

I will give thanks and praise to You, for I am fearfully and wonderfully made; Wonderful are Your works, and my soul knows it very well.
Psalm 139:14

Chapter Fifty-Six
Magic Eight

All horses deserve, at least once in their lives, to be loved by a little girl.
Unknown

  I was 110% convinced I'd have girls and they'd enter the world holding a Breyer's horse in their hands, which from a birthing perspective would be awful. We'd play horses instead of Hot Wheels and they would love horses as much as I do. Well, I have amazing sons who tolerate my horse craziness, and life is good. No complaints, only blessings there.
  Luckily for me, my friend Nicole has a horse-crazy girl she

occasionally shares with me, and the fabulousness that is her girl Blakely gives me that fix. There is literally nothing more fun in the world than talking horses with a young girl. Remember being that horse crazy girl? Me too. Like it was yesterday. Or today, even. She's eight. The perfect age for magic and belief; the perfect ingredients for the best kind of horse connection.

Blakely was coming over to see my horses and I was excited and nervous. All morning I was wondering what would an eight-year-old girl care to hear or see from an adult she barely knows? I felt the pressure of my desire to somehow distill the essence of why those of us on this journey care so much. It felt so important to help her see a glimpse into the magic of horses, which we overlook and oppress so often, and which too many of us have learned the hard way. From the do-it-as-wrong-as-possible way, only to realize that what you'd really like most is to find your way back to how you were when you too were eight.

Blakely arrived wearing a bright pink coat. It's hard to go too far wrong with anything when you look adorable and are the magic age of eight. All my thoughts of what to say fell away, so I just told her she was the best age in the whole world and that she has all the advantage over adults. She smiled at me like I'd confirmed something she already knew. I told her that for some reason adults get all weird and worried and unfun with horses and have to relearn all the things that she already knows. She smiled again like she already knew how weird and worried adults can be.

I told her she's right in the heart of horse magic time and that I'm pretty darn sure horses love eight-year-old girls the most. My horse friends often talk about how we wish we could rewind to how we were with horses before we let adulthood get a hold of us. Blakely smiled, possibly humoring me, but I told her she can skip all of that because she is that girl right now.

"You love horses, like I do, right?" I asked, and her face broke out in a shy affirming smile. "What do you like most?" I asked, and she had to think because, well, because horses. She said, "Everything." It was my turn to smile.

"Me too, Blakely. Me too."

We chatted about the lessons she's taking, the horse she's riding (Sugar), and how much she loves it all. We talked about what it's like from the moment she arrives at the stable, to the moment she goes to get her horse. We talked about how horses like to make choices just like we do. We talked about how honoring those choices and working to get our choices going together was the key to a good relationship with your horse. I asked if she got excited when she was on her way to the stable and the answer was clear by the sparkle in her eyes. I asked who her best friend was (her Mom; oh I miss those days) and to imagine how much excitement and energy comes out of us when we get to see someone we really enjoy. We talked about how Sugar would like to feel the same way, and to feel it from us. We talked about how to show Sugar her efforts are recognized and appreciated, especially since she's a lesson horse. We talked of how horses touch each other differently than what we tend to do. We practiced the curved, firm, but gentle fingers that mimic a nuzzle and about how Sugar might like a wither scratch or two.

    I asked her if she'd ever smelled a horse, really smelled one, and she looked at me like I was a bit crazy but like she wanted to really smell a horse, too. We agreed it's the best smell in the world, but that we'd smell politely; that neither horses nor humans appreciate a stranger coming in for a stolen sniff. I was so glad Simba was still with me so that she could experience the wonder of that wise horse. Blakely introduced herself to him, like we'd talked about…silently saying hello and seeing what happened next.

    They stood together in silent conversation, and shortly Simba's head came to rest near her knee as they made friends. I could see the thoughts cross her mind as she gently stood off to his side and ever so gently approached him to nestle her nose in his fuzzy neck. She took her time and when she stood back with a smile on her face, I knew that yep, eight is a magic number.

    All horses should be so lucky as to experience the love, the wonder, the magic of being loved by a young girl. Blakely is my reminder that there's still a young horse crazy girl inside of all of us not-always-young-women who love horses just as much as we ever did.

And if you're one of those women, honor that young horse girl buried inside of you. Get in front of the nearest mirror (I know, I know, but DO it), take a deep breath and blow it out. Blow out all the cobwebs, the dust, the disappointments, the discouragement, the crap that life likes to plop on your plate. Blow it out like a birthday candle.

Close your eyes, breathe again, and see if you can see that girl now.

Wait there until your eyes start to sparkle, your heart lifts, and you want nothing more than to throw on your boots, run out the door to the nearest horse and bury your nose in that intoxicating smell.

Bring your young girl back and polish her off. Don't let anybody shut her down or put a you-know-what in her punchbowl. That eight-year-old girl inside all of us and your horse will thank you for it.

Much too soon it was time for them to go. I think I had more fun than Blakely did. As we said our goodbyes, I asked Blakely if she had a favorite color horse. This one she said, this color is my favorite. I smiled, because Blakely hit it right on the head. It's something we grown-ups too often forget.

The best color horse is the one you're with.

Chapter Fifty-Seven
I've Got You

Being seen, being heard, feeling felt, and getting gotten.
Sarah Schlote

Have you ever played what if? Sometimes when our sons were young, we'd play a version called "What would we do if there was a zombie apocalypse?" Fortunately, those are exactly the kind of life skills video games help develop. We'd run through scenarios of what we'd do to survive and pick who we'd want on our team. Let me tell you, it stings if you're picked last for the survival team—kind of like dodgeball all over again. I'd pick Pat for sure, every time. He's got the skills to handle it.

Fortunately, most days we don't need to run zombie survival scenarios through our heads; we're just trying to make it through a day filled with a zillion daily kinds of things. Chores, life's usual stressors, highs and lows. Not apocalyptic, but exhausting. Before you even realize it's happening, you can find yourself running on fumes and dreaming that someone would swoop in and clean the house, make dinner, rub your feet—something to take the load off. Here, my biggest load is the animal farm; trying to get out of town with five horses, two wild dogs, and a cat isn't easy. Having a good house/animal sitter is a big deal. Ours had moved and I was having a hard time finding someone for a trip out of town. My son Jake had called and I was telling him my animal woes. He heard the wobble in my voice and said, "Mom, I've got you. I can do this; you guys need to get out of town."

I almost bawled. Those words, "I've got you," struck me right in the heart. Such little words but they pack such a huge impact. I've got your back; I'm there for you; no worries. My eyes welled up at the kindness and support of those words, delivered by someone who knows me and loves me and yep, somebody who's looking out for me. After hearing "I've got you" from Jake, it dawned on me how awesome it would be if our horses felt "I've got you" from us. Too often we bring the messy weight of our busy lives to our time with them, thinking about other things rather than soaking up the quiet exchange we can have together. What horses want to feel from us is the same I felt from Jake—I've got you. Horses are at their essence comfort seekers. They want to know we've got them. That they can count on us not to lose our minds on them. My goal with True is that he knows whatever we do, wherever we go, my goal is to be the person he would want on his zombie apocalypse team.

Chapter Fifty-Eight
Soft Heart in a Hard World

*A friend is someone who knows the song in your heart,
and can sing it back to you when you forget the words.
Unknown*

    My phone buzzed in my pocket; it was my very dear friend, having a very tough time. I don't always get good reception, so I was grateful her voice came through loud and clear. Half the time I'm talking to someone, I lose them even when I'm standing still and it makes me want to make a tinfoil hat to get better reception. Rural broadband, need I say more? I know how it feels when you really need someone to pick up the other end of the line. Sometimes all we can do is listen. Listening is so underrated in our fast world. We like to hear our own voices and when others are talking, we're thinking of what we want to say next. Guilty. As I listened, the words I heard were so harsh. Not to me, but the words she used to describe herself. All too often we pose our words to others (and ourselves) as if we're asking permission to feel what we do. Asking for approval, for validation. Labeling ourselves in diminishing ways. Ouch. She's not alone.

We've been friends forever and it hurt my heart to hear how hard she was on herself. Life can be hard enough without punching our own selves in the head. We talked until the words she needed to say had been said. Then it was my turn to find what I wanted to say. "This is what I know," I said. "You haven't gotten this far in life by being a lightweight. You haven't earned the bumps and bruises and scars scattered across your body and your life by not showing up. You've showed up plenty. You've stood up. Grappled with tough times. You've won some, some have taken their toll, but you're still in the game. Being tired under the strain is not weak. Feeling at the end of your rope does not make you a failure, it makes you human."

We cried; we laughed. We felt better. We were hours apart, but it didn't matter. No matter where our friends are, good friends always have ears to hear. Good friends see the best in us, help us be the best in us. This day it was my turn to be there for her; other days, she's the one who talks me off the ledge. Friends are the family we weren't born with. We choose them, and they choose us. We take turns cheering each other on. It's a win-win-win. I'm so grateful for the blessing of wonderful friends in my life. Friends are there for the all of it; the good, the bad, the ugly. Wiping the sweat from your face, bringing you water. Or a margarita.

Most of all, friends remind you that you've kept your heart soft in a hard world.

That alone is an act of courage.

Chapter Fifty-Nine
Last Horse, a Poem

I smile when I catch God watching me through the eyes of a horse.
Kevin Weatherby

    Just yesterday a friend shared a picture of her beautiful new horse on Facebook. She'd lost a horse not long ago, and had searched far to find her new girl. Someone asked her how old her new horse was, and she wrote, "She's five; she's my last horse." Oof. Reality bites sometimes. Social media can be a minefield, for sure, but it's also created wonderful opportunities to connect with other horse lovers all around the world. It's been such a blessing to hear from people who love horses as much as I do, and to share the joys and the sorrows of loving a horse.

After I lost Simba this year I received such kindness from people who've also known that pain. Deciding what to do after losing a horse is tough. Do you bring a new horse into your life? As you age, should you stop thinking about young horses? Any horses? I've heard from so many people who are at a point in their lives where they wonder how many more years doing such a thing even "makes sense." This poem came to me one day after reading a particularly poignant message from an older woman who shared with me how sad she was after losing her horse and she had begun thinking that she really shouldn't even think of looking for another at her age.

I wrote this for her, and all of us animal lovers who may someday think the same.

Last Horse
This is my last horse, she told me,
Softly first, and then with gusto
Last horse, last dog, last cat, for that matter,
last whatever might outlive me, she said
I'm for damn sure not getting a tortoise
or a donkey
no matter how cute he might be

So a goldfish, maybe, I don't know
I can see the tipping scale; days ahead less than my days behind
I did the math and it comes up short
Too short to think of any more,
of the responsibility
of another life
a heartbeat other than mine

So that's that,
And this was it, she said
her last horse, forever.
No more colts or projects or mustangs
Mustangs she said, Good Lord help me
Man, I was full of mustang dreams in the day

They're much like me she said, must be why I love them so
And project horses, man, they always got me she said
Crying out for someone to see, to feel their pain, to hear their voices
Well, I heard, she said,
and I never could say no to them
Busted and broken and grateful,
oh so grateful
But they blessed me more than I ever blessed them
Funny how that is

And so they came into her life
not just horses but others too,
dogs and cats, a potbellied pig
(his name was Sam)
Anything that needed a home
They came too
and stayed forever
for however long forever was

There were no one night stands with her
No passing whims of fancy
Once you were in, well, you were in it to the end
Together
The good the beautiful the heartbreaking
The joyous hellos and the gut-punch goodbyes
the all of it
She'd seen her share of love and loss
No light-weight love for her
But big love, lots of it, doled out with a generous heart, nothing held back
The kind of love that leaves you bare
bare but happy
Oh so happy
A lifetime of it,

She blinked at the sudden pool that'd caught in her lashes

She paused, caught her breath,
and looked at me with a challenge in her eye
And, she said, again, with gusto, to be sure I got it,
I'm selling my saddle too

Well hell I thought
I'd heard her words and felt the weight
of a lifetime of hope
and dreams
and horses,
always horses
Of animals she'd loved and who'd loved her back,
no matter what

Not fickle like people can be,
but clear and true like animals do
Her words lingered there, hanging in the air between us
as if gravity held no weight right then
Maybe this is how dreams fall, I thought?
Hung out to dry, hitting the ground, dying,
if no one's there to catch them,
or if no one knows they should
if no one reaches out to hold them aloft when gravity calls?

I felt the challenge and the question in her eyes
What would I do with the words she'd shared?
Would I nod my head and agree
Yes, that's right, you're an old woman
(or soon to be),
enough with these childish things
prepare yourself for that gray future, that's the thing to do
You're right to say No more, be done with all that
Good sense should prevail
Anyone with any sense would say the same,

It's time

Pull back, scale down,
love less, care less,
try less, right?
Well, I was the wrong person then,
and maybe just maybe, she already knew that
Maybe she was trying it out on me,
like new jeans to see how it fit

Not today, I thought,
Tinker Bell's not dying on my watch, woman
So no, I said, hold up, would ya?
How do we know, really,
when that day will be?
Look at me, I'm not the one to ask
I went out for a ride one day thinking I'd be back for dinner
Well look how that turned out
We are not the Captain of our days, and that's fine by me
We have right now
and that's what counts

And so Yea, I said, maybe no more 4-year olds or mustangs,
but there will always be
someone who's lost
something,
A leg, an eye, a home, a chance
You can scoop them up
in your new time of life
You can still be so much
do so much

Be the soft place to land
For those no one wants
the blind, the aged,
the mangy,
the ugly
For them,

because they will always need
a forever home,
for however long forever is

Don't let time stop you I said
Time's only a thief if we let it be,
snuggle them into your wheelchair,
tuck the blind cat on the seat of your walker when you go to get your glass of wine,
tuck them into your bed at night, gently, like feathers falling
Find a friend, a partner in crime, ask the little horse crazy girl, there's always one of those, that will always be true
to help you feed carrots to that moon blind horse no one else wanted

Let your last horse be the white one, the one who comes to you in your last dream
as you say goodbye to your life here
and catch that final ride to God's side
This isn't your last horse, it's not your last anything, your heart is too beautiful for lasts like that,
and anyway, just for what it's worth,
I'm banking on the fact that God loves horses too.

For Simba and Deb

Chapter Sixty
Lucky Charms

They're magically delicious.

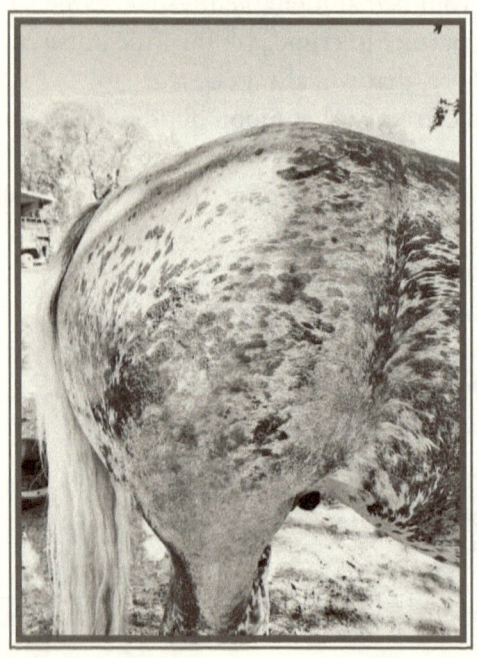

    Was I the only kid whose mom didn't let them eat sugary cereal? My Mom didn't believe in good-tasting cereal. She was committed to keeping me healthy. That meant I was eating Grape Nuts and cardboard-flavored bran cereals while it seemed like all my friends were eating Lucky Charms. One of the best part of sleepovers was getting to eat their cereal. My Mom was serious about it, but I wasn't completely deprived. She kept a small box of Captain Crunch tucked away in the pantry, for special occasions like days I had sleep-overs. She innately knew that no one would ever come back if she served them Raisin Bran the next morning, and I was grateful for that. Disclaimer: Lucky Charms were delicious but Captain Crunch was the BEST. It was so good (maybe it was but it tore the crud out of your mouth). Do you remember that? Somewhere a sadistic cereal maker is laughing at all the kids with bloody gums.

Sometimes when I have an "aha!" moment with True where everything clicks, it feels like we found a little horsemanship nugget that fits right where there'd been a missing part. It reminds me of how rewarding it was to find those little crunchy marshmallow charms after digging through the rest of the cereal. Those Lucky Charm moments are rare, but so sweet.

Turns out my Mom was right again, of course. She was ahead of the times on the importance of nutritional breakfasts. One cup of Captain Crunch has sixteen grams of sugar, Grape Nuts five. It makes me feel sorry for all the teachers when sugared-up kids have a mid-morning blood sugar crash.

Chapter Sixty-One
Dreams

*Don't sell your saddle, don't give up on dreams.
Take time to see them through,
there are no easy trails,
hard work makes dreams come true.
You'll make it through the tough times,
friends will stick like glue.
Don't ever sell your saddle.
Dreams won't give up on you.
Don Bishop*

After my wreck, I wanted to ride again, but wasn't sure if I'd be able to. Physically or mentally. But it was a dream that wouldn't die. I didn't want it to die. And one day, thanks to Simba the wonder horse's kind invitation, I was able to swing that first leg over and to get back in that saddle. It was a dream that did come true.

Do we even have time for such things as dreams these fraught days? The last few years have sat on us like a big fat elephant, individually and collectively. Does it feel frivolous even, to talk about dreams right now? We're navigating the impacts of such huge issues: the pandemic, homelessness, fire, drought, fighting with each other about hoarding toilet paper, so talking about dreams sounds kinda like fluff. But without hope, which is what dreams are built on, we become weary. Our resilience, to deal not only with whatever trials come before us, but to stand strong emotionally and spiritually without growing defeated depends in good part on our emotional bandwidth. That internal something where we find our strength, our refreshment, the juice to get up and do it all over AGAIN even when there's every reason we should be weary to the bone. I think that's where dreams come in.

Maybe it makes more sense to call it our passion—what is it that makes our eyes shine, our heart beat faster, joy run through our veins? How often can you say you've felt any of those things lately? But, we need to. I know what it feels like to look in the mirror and see that your eyes have lost their shine. The face looking back at me looked like a sad stranger. It scared me, scared me enough to do something about it. It happens, often without us even realizing it is. If your eyes have lost that shine, it's usually a really good clue you're running on empty. That's the time an intervention is called for, to call on a friend who'll stand in the gap for you. A friend who will pray with you and for you, cry with you, laugh with you, and if need be, bring the shovel and ask where you want the body buried. Find a friend who sees the beautiful you down under the dust. I've been blessed to have those friends, the ones who saw me going dim and came over with coffee and a big old dust rag to dust me off and get me re-booted.

Life is a road filled with beautiful vistas as well as pot holes.

We all have those times where we fall into those pot holes. We've pulled ourselves out of them, rims bent a bit, tires a little low on air—but we do it. We may be a little bedraggled but we do it, and dreams can help us keep our eyes pointed forward. So take good care of those dreams. They are the stuff of magic. Cherish them, for they help keep that light in your eyes. The world needs all the light we can share.

After all, the most interesting of us have been broken and mended and broken again.
Jenny Lawson

Chapter Sixty-Two
Let Go

Let it all go. See what stays.
Osho

What if we…
Let go.
Let go of holding on so tightly.
Holding on to the end of the lead rope, the end of control, of trying to force something to be somewhere it's not yet able to be.
Let go of expectations.
Those that don't serve you or your horse, or anyone, really.

Let go of fear.
Fix what we can, look what we can't straight in the eye and walk through it, or around it, and be done with it.

What if we…let go of waiting.
The time is now, not yesterday or tomorrow.
Life is happening now.
Let go of all that keeps us tied up.
Imagine how that would feel?
All the driving, the forcing, trying to shove the square peg in a round hole.
It won't go ya know?
Let it go.
Stop the hamster wheel in our heads and breathe.
Breathe again. And one more time.
Close our eyes, shake out the visions and stories that don't serve us well.
Let go of those hard eyes and try out soft eyes.
Feel what it feels like to breathe and just be.
Let go of the armor, the barriers that don't serve us well, that keep our bodies tied up in knots.
We've let go of driving our horses around like kites on the end of a string, but we're still doing it to ourselves.

What if we…
Let go of those hard fists and let our fingers open, let go of whatever needs to be let go of, at the ready to catch anything that needs to be caught within those spaces laced with grace.
Step off into that space where only faith exists and you'll find that you will not fall.
Grace will not fail you.
In that space of acceptance all our gifts can flourish; not constrained by anger, fear, worry and control.
But with wide open hearts; wide open to what is.
Step off into the space where Grace exists.

Chapter Sixty-Three
When Things get Western

Between stimulus and response there is a space. In that space is our power to choose our response.
In our response lies our growth and our freedom.
Victor E. Frankl

Charley Snell helped me understand that our horses need to know us as a place of peace. But any of us who've experienced when things go south in the great "out there," we know things aren't always peaceful. That's the flip side of being there for our horses, how we help our horse be prepared to handle those "when things get western" situations. If you haven't heard that term before, well, it's when you-know-what hits the fan. When things get real, real fast. For me, it was a case of real western when I started on this journey. I'd attended my very first clinic with my young gelding Skeeter. Just getting to the clinic involved me driving my kids up to Oregon so my folks could watch them, making a fast U-turn to drive back to California, loading Skeeter up, and driving another four hours to the clinic. In spite of all the back and forthing, I was excited/terrified. Bright eyed and bushy-tailed so to speak, naïve as all get out, and excited to learn "stuff."

Well, turns out the first thing I learned was that all saddles are not created equal, and that it's pretty darn important that your saddle actually fits the horse you're riding. Skeeter and I saddled up, entered the arena, and he proceeded to buck on a perfect diagonal the entire length of the arena. Quite a way to make an entrance. I'd advise against it. I wrote about this in *Broken, Tales of a Titanium Cowgirl* and I would like to mention again that I recall my hand in the air, riding that buck. My friend Stephanie was there and she'll attest to it. Such a proud moment (insert face palm emoji here).

Balance is the challenge, as it always is, in horsemanship and life! Some of us find it easy to be peaceful and move carefully around our horses but harder to maintain calm when things get a little wonky. If our horse spooks telling us, OH NO, LOOK AT THAT! and we join in with, HOLY CRAP, YOU'RE RIGHT, THAT'S TERRIFYING! well, that's a problem. There are also people much more comfortable with noisy business; sometimes skipping over the "place of peace" entirely. If our horse says, OH NO, I CAN'T DO THAT and we join in with, YES YOU CAN AND I'LL ESCALATE THIS MOTHER TILL YOU CAN, well, that's a problem.

Depending on how we've learned along the way, we can tend to land heavy on one side or the other. We've all seen videos of people flopping every conceivable item at a horse with the intention of getting that horse used to anything and everything, including flying monkeys. The unintended consequence of the too-much approach is that some horses will show their overwhelm by blowing up, while others may turn inward to escape the overload. There's an unintended consequence of tip-toeing around, as well, and it comes up when (not if) something in the "great out there" happens and our horse's mind leaves the building. If we don't develop that side of our relationship, as well, big gaps can show up when things get western. Rather than work on helping our horse develop confidence in us and themselves, we can tiptoe, and I know I did that with Wish. Instead of going there, building those confidence muscles, we can find ourselves riding around thinking, "Boy, I hope this holds together until I get off!" Nobody wants an unintended dismount. Been there, done that.

It's kind of like Goldilocks and the Three Bears. The secret is arriving at just the right spot; but without breaking and entering like she did. It seems like in all things in life and horses, there's a fine line. Between being a place of peace, and also being somebody your horse would choose for Team Zombie Apocalypse, or otherwise known as Team When Things get Western. Because the goal is that our horses learn to think through things themselves, learning in an environment of trust and safety. That when something unexpected happens, we don't escalate it but help them navigate through it, building confidence in the process. We'll never be able to get a horse "used" to everything including UFOs, but we can help them trust we will walk with them through scary stuff until they believe they, too, can face zombies.

Chapter Sixty-Four
Little Things

*Everybody needs beauty as well as bread, places to play in and pray in,
where nature may heal and give strength to body and soul alike.*
John Muir

When the world feels crazy, sometimes it helps to go back to basics.

Show up.

Do your best.

Tell the truth.

Breathe.

Let go of the outcome.

Chapter Sixty-Five
Truth Serum

Write the truest sentence you know.
Ernest Hemingway

Sounds easy, right? Well, it's not, let me tell you. I learned this the hard way when I hosted a writer's clinic I titled Truth Serum, with the charge to write as Hemingway encouraged. It sounded like such a great topic, until I sat down and pondered what that really looked like. Writers have a need to find a home for the words that bubble up inside them. Words they feel compelled to share with the world, even though writing with your heart on your sleeve, writing the truth, the bold truth of your feelings and observations is a terrifying position to willingly place yourself in. You put your heart on the page and then hand it out for someone else's eyes, someone else's heart, to read and interpret. That can be a very vulnerable place. After *Broken* was published, I thought, what have I done? I didn't want to write all the thoughts churning around in my heart into a journal, yet I wrote it in a book and sent it out for the world to see? Of course, the only people who see those words are people who felt interested enough to read or listen to my book, but still. I'll never forget that feeling of sending it out into the world, and then wondering what the heck I'd just done, like one of those dreams you have where you find yourself at a potluck, where instead of bringing a dish to share, a seven-layer Jell-O salad perhaps, you showed up nude.

Brené Brown talks about the power of vulnerability. It's kind of sad that we needed a ground-breaking pioneer to tell us that being authentic, that speaking the truth from our hearts, is really the best way. The best way to develop full, deep, honest, funny, profound, heart-breaking, up- lifting, encouraging, supportive, solid relationships and bonds us with each other. It's a deeply life-affirming realization when we realize a powerful freedom comes in being authentic; and in finding others who honor that effort, we feel seen and heard for who we are. It's ridiculous that it takes a stranger who has spent her or his life studying this, this that should be Life 101, to tell us so. To encourage us to be brave. To be vulnerable. To speak the truth of ourselves.

This is the beauty of horses. They see right through us. They already know these things. Maybe not know, in the cognitive sense we think, but know through their DNA, through their history on this planet. Horses live in the space of now. Of the moment, of the truth of what the environment is telling them reading the energy, the landscape, and responding accordingly. Not only for survival, but for relationship with each other. For some reason they've offered us the grace to form relationships with them. Two creatures; one that shows its feelings through its motions and the other (us) who hides them.

How do we find a way to speak to each other? We're dissembling sorts, with others and with ourselves, and shying away from saying what we really think, what we really feel, asking for what we really need. And yet, that is the space horses open up for us, and more often than not we step into that interface still holding tight to the baggage and bondage and all the nonsense that's been conditioned into us. And while we're standing there, holding tight to all that stuff, our horses are saying, "Hey you, you can go ahead and put that down. In fact, I wish you would."

What a responsibility. What an opportunity. What a gift.

Chapter Sixty-Six
I Water This Tree

Great things are done by a series of small things brought together.
Vincent Van Gogh

    Talking to my friends about what we've experienced these past few crazy years, it feels like we're all sharing a sense of cognitive dissonance. The pandemic, economy, fires, drought, aging parents, empty nests, polarizing politics, social concerns…the list goes on. We're all searching for ways to make sense of incredibly hard things. Sometimes the weight of it feels too heavy for our heads and hearts. Sometimes it's the simple, small things, which make the most sense to me. These words came to me as I was doing chores. I hope they speak to you like they did to me. Never doubt that even our small efforts are steps in the right direction.

I water this tree.
When I don't know what else to do, I water this tree.
When I'm doing my chores, changing the horses' water, I say you look thirsty
and this tree says yes I am.
So I water this tree.
I say good job you for withstanding this drought, sometimes all you can do is endure, and you're doing it. Let me help you, I know it's just a bit.
I save crickets.
I have a special cricket saving set-up, a postcard and a red Solo cup.
I call it Move yo' cricket.
I dust around spiders.
I feed Daisy and Oliver the raven couple dog food I buy special for them.
When they ask for seconds, I feed them again.
I pick up rocks in the arena.
One less rock to stumble upon.
I try to reuse plastic and try to use less, all the way around.
I try to be kind.
I try to smile and say hey, I see you fellow traveler, navigating this wild and wooly trail.
I see you, you are not alone.
This is me, living a small life in a small place, but it feels big to me.
Fire drought politics hate.
They're beyond my purview and beyond anything I can change, but I can water this tree.
I can save crickets.
I can dust around spiders.
I can pray.

I can breathe.
I can believe that love conquers hate.
Our efforts may seem so small as to not make a difference, but I don't believe that.
So I water this tree.

Chapter Sixty-Seven
Horses and Zebras

When you hear hoofbeats, think horses, not zebras.
Dr. Theodore E. Woodward

(Or, when you finally get the diagnosis explaining why you've felt like crap for most of a year....)

In medicine, a good diagnosis is often based on the old quote, "When you hear hoofbeats, think horses, not zebras." A skilled doctor uses reasoning to rule out most likely ailments first before resorting to chasing more rare and exotic maladies. I'd heard this phrase at least a hundred times when I was working in research. Funny how I couldn't recall it at all in trying to figure out what was wrong with my aching body. I'd been chasing zebras for months. I'd been feeling all kinds of weird pains in my right hip (yeah, the leg that's supposed to go over the saddle) that moved around and slowed me down. The first diagnosis I received was a strained sartorius, then piriformis syndrome, then whacked out hip flexors. It was frustrating, and painful. Throwing a leg over True became less and less possible, so my work with him moved to the ground. The pain was weird. Sometimes intermittent, sometimes acute, always moving, and finally, settling into a dull ache. Chronic pain takes its toll on you physically and mentally. I've watched friends suffer from chronic pain that sidelines them from doing the things they love to do. Chronic pain is often silent-suffering because until you've experienced it, you really don't appreciate what a toll it takes.

The pandemic really took a toll on our health care system; it's so overwhelmed right now. It takes time to march through all the steps to be seen. I feel for all those in healthcare trying to help others, and keep themselves sane at the same time. Finally, I had a Physical Therapy assessment with someone I know and respect. He put me through all the moves and said, "Well, I think it's your hip." I like Joe a lot but I was thinking, Um, no @#$% Sherlock. But what Joe meant, and what I'd never even imagined, was that my hip joint itself was wasted. He used nicer words than that, but the X-Ray he ordered confirmed that I was now in the category of people needing new parts. I thought new hips were the purview of grandparents, but it turned out that all that pain was due to worn out parts and I wasn't immune just because I don't have grandkids. Yet. That's my secret signal to know if my sons read this or not. Turns out it was a horse staring me in the face all along, I just couldn't see it. When my very kind doctor called to confirm the news, I said a very bad word and started bawling. Fortunately, he's a friend, as well, and he forgave me.

After we hung up, I cried, gnashed my teeth, ate a cookie, and Googled "Can you ride after a hip replacement?" The first thing that popped up was an article in *Horse and Rider* interviewing three people who got back in the saddle lickety-split. Oh good, I thought,

I believe everything these people say and stopped Googling. Turns out there's a whole world of bionic people riding around like crazy. The Internet, as always, is simultaneously terrifying and comforting. I wasn't anxious to have any more bionic parts; I was hoping to keep my first go-round of titanium parts a one-off. Although eleven years had passed, I wasn't ready to be taken apart only to be put back together one more time. Trauma is sneaky. Even though I felt I'd come through the trauma of my wreck, there was a residue left and I could feel it surfacing. I really, really didn't want this to be true, and my emotions were really committed to wanting the rest of my body keeping its original parts. But hallelujah for the audacity of medicine, neurosurgeons, and orthopedic surgeons. I didn't want new parts, but I was blessed that I could get new parts.

And so, my new adventure in bionic parts began. I drove myself to my first consultation and hobbled through the parking lot. The waiting room was filled with people in Crocs and cargo shorts. I looked around and thought, these are my people now. People whose pain has driven them to comfortable shoes and practical pants. At my first consult I told the very nice surgeon, "I hate orthopedic surgery; it sounds horrible and saws are creepy." He side-eyed me trying to process just how weird I was and said, "Um, well, you'll be asleep." I told him yeah, but I know what goes down in there, so there. It felt important to let the second surgeon know I was vehemently opposed to surgeries that required saws and mallets and he smiled and said, "I get it," but he, too, reminded me I'd be out of it.

Once again, it was up to me to process my new "story." Not broken per se, but in serious need of replacement parts. The words "rode hard and put up wet" took up unbidden residence in my head, an ironic reminder of how I'd failed to see the hoof prints all over this and sought a hundred zebras instead. Finally, I had an answer to the story of why I'd been feeling less-than for most of the year, and finally, a direction to point after feeling frustrated and without a way forward. But now that we'd identified that it was a "horse" and not a zebra I'd been chasing I knew which way I had to go. No part of me wanted to head back to the operating room again. No one does. But I wanted to move forward so that once again, I could find my way back to the saddle. My friend Richard often says "the more things change, the more they remain the same." In the case of me and my bones he's right; I'm going in for new parts, once again.

    P.S. The surgical booklet they gave me has a photo of a very nice-looking older gentleman wearing really bad golf shoes on the cover. When the surgical coordinator asked if I had the booklet I said, yes, I do, but I think all of us would feel a little bit better about this process if you gave that nice man some better-looking golf shoes.

Chapter Sixty-Eight
Bilateral Blues

Life should not be a journey to the grave with the intention of arriving safely in a pretty and well-preserved body, but rather to skid in broadside in a cloud of smoke, thoroughly used up, totally worn out, and loudly proclaiming "Wow! What a Ride!"
Hunter S. Thompson

Funny how we're cruising along in life and then plop, into the valley we go. Finding out that my hip was a mess knocked the wind out of my sails. The next day I still felt a bit like a tree had landed on me, when I got one of those calls you never want to receive; the thing we've been dreading happened—my sweet little Mom had fallen and broken her hip. Her health has been a roller coaster ride the last two years, speeding along gathering up speed downhill, without the fun adrenaline rush part. Her health had been suffering since her stroke seven years ago. I'd been having that impending doom feeling, so worried that she'd break something during one of her frequent falls. My folks were five hours away from home when it happened, trying to have an enjoyable little getaway. My Dad was fending for the both of them, navigating the landscape of now what, and finally getting an emergency surgery scheduled. My heart hurt for her, for him, for all of us. It hurts my heart to see how hard these years have been on her, and in spite of it, she's been a warrior. My Mom's taken to saying, "I don't recommend getting old." I've taken to replying, "So, should I just die now?" It makes her smile, because she loves even the sarcastic me.

While I'd been worrying about my Mom's health, Pat had been worrying about me. Now, at least we had a diagnosis that my right hip is an, excuse me, fudged up mess. My Mom and I were sharing a painful symmetry. Who knows how or when our parts wear out? Nature? Nurture? Lack of nurture? It may be trauma-related from my accident, and may be just wear and tear from living life. Bones seem to be my thing and now my hip was joining the list of the broken and busted. When life feels like it's sitting heavy on my chest, I go outside. There's something about fresh air and trees that seems to put things into perspective. The horses were peacefully munching the expensive hay we've had to scrounge in this grinding drought. It's such a comforting sound I decided to do a peg-leg crawl through the fence and plopped down on the salt block next to True as he was eating. He turned to get a sense of what weirdness I was up to, determined I was pretty innocuous sitting on the salt block, and kept eating.

Our bodies are fascinating. One half of my body felt just fine, awesome even, and the right side, well, it felt traitorous. It's a weird feeling, like you're two separate parts. I've already got two strikes against me; first, I'm an only child and we all know how they are. Second, I'm a Gemini, the astrological sign of the twins which have been described as, "their personality doesn't allow much depth." Ouch. If I paid attention to astrology, I'd be feeling pretty crappy about myself, but I'm going to guess the guy who wrote it is a Virgo. Astrological humor. My best friend's a Virgo so we really are a pair. But as I sat on that salt block, I felt such a dichotomy. Maybe I am a Gemini girl, split right down the middle. Twins, in one body. One of the downfalls of being bilaterally symmetrical, perhaps, like people and snails are. Sometimes your two sides are feeling like one whole, and other times one of them just goes off the rails and you find yourself sitting on a salt block. I know I am not the only one feeling like life catches up with you. Most of my friends and horse people I know have gotten banged up over time and are feeling a little worse for wear. We hobble around but we're all united in wanting to get patched up and get back in the saddle. For me, it would be my second go round, finding the way forward as I tried to put my body and mind back together to ride again. I picked myself up off that salt block and brushed bits of hay off the well-worn jeans I was wearing. I love old jeans. The more worn the better. We love jeans that are worn in just right, but we don't apply that same concept to our own aging too often. As I looked down at my knees I thought, gosh, we're going through the same process, becoming like our favorite jeans. Showing the wear and tear of life, but gaining a patina that has its own kind of shine. Sometimes faded, whiskered in a few places (take that as you will), but also comfortable, just right.

    We all have our favorites; the jeans you reach for, the ones that make you sad when the knees finally blow out. Or in my case, hip. The ones that once you slip them on, you feel like the very best you. It's kind of weird that the more worn they are, the more we love them. None of us have the luxury of life untouched. As I straightened out my angry leg, I looked down at my favorite jeans and thought, jeans, you're my new inspiration. Kind of like life. Hunter S. Thompson was a larger-than-life character and said many things, some of them flat out nuts, but this one speaks to all of us who love horses more than unblemished bodies. "Life should not be a journey to the grave with the intention of arriving safely in a pretty and well-preserved body, but rather to skid in broadside in a cloud of smoke, thoroughly used up, totally worn out, and loudly proclaiming 'Wow! What a Ride!'"

Chapter Sixty-Nine
Déjà vu

Plus ça change, plus c'est la même chose.
Jean-Baptiste Alphonse Karr

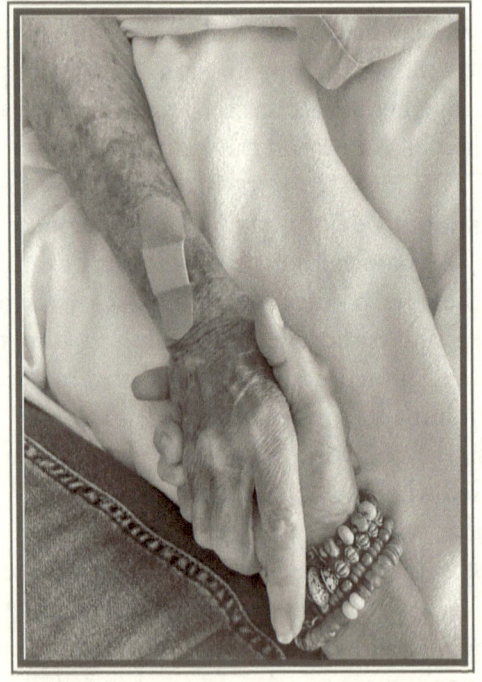

The more things change, the more they remain the same.
Life is weird. I'm feeling a huge sense of been there, done that. Eleven years after my accident with Wish, and I'm going in for a second go-round of titanium parts. Last time, I remember those five days in ICU waiting for surgery and wondering how it would all turn out. This time, my surgery's scheduled weeks out as it's not the result of an accident, just parts wearing out. Each day I wait adds a

little more anxiety to my feelings about the whole deal. This diagnosis has been a struggle for me to accept. When I was little there were so many things I wanted to be when I grew up; but unfortunately, I didn't turn out to be a comedic tap dancing veterinarian. I had no idea I'd be none of those but that instead I'd become more and more bionic each decade. It would be a lot more fun to be a tap dancer than someone who sets airport alarms off.

And it wasn't just me experiencing major life shifts, it was my Mom, as well. Last time I was looking at titanium parts my grandmother was in a painful decline. This time, instead of holding my grandmother's hands, I find myself holding my mother's as she's recovering from surgery to repair her broken hip. It's an odd symmetry and I don't like it. Her break created a double-whammy to her health which has been challenged by the erosive nature of the cognitive and physical ramifications set in play from her stroke years before. My Mom has dementia. Vascular dementia, to be specific. These are the small delineations you come to care about when someone you love has been slapped upside the face with such a diagnosis. And though we all had such hopes that she would make a complete comeback, the years since have been unkind. There are many ways to lose someone. Some are harsh and fast, some are expected, and others are more like the relentless drip of water on a rock over time.

It's hard watching the passage of time eat away at those we love. It sucks. So many of my friends also are watching their parents' and grandparents' health decline. If you've experienced it, you know it isn't for the faint of heart. It's a balancing act of emotions, watching the people we know and love so well come in and out of focus, trying to find the best way to be there for them, and setting aside our expectations of how we wish things were. Sometimes it feels like death by 1000 paper cuts. There's little I can do but be a support, as best I can. I can still recall the feeling of holding my grandmother's paper-thin hand in mine, but now, years later, holding my Mom's hand, there's a too painful symmetry I'd happily skip.

My Mom and I now do the same as I remember doing with my grandmother eleven years ago. We, too, talk about the past, zigzagging from warm memories, comfortable topics, to occasional outliers. I try to keep up the best I can. When she tells me she's in England or France and that it's cold there, I smile and say "better wear a sweater," and she agrees. I hold her hand and wait until we come back to the now. There's also beauty in the past, sweet recollections of her childhood, my grandparents, and how she felt when she first became a mom. She tells me of the day she and my father brought me home; how unsure she felt, but at the same time, filled with such an overwhelming love for me. I'm her only, and she's my only too. Somehow in spite of the sterile and sometimes chaotic environment of her recovery room, we've found a place of remembered happiness where we find moments of solace in spite of the circumstances. I record her words as she talks, as I never want to forget how her voice sounds when she tells me these things. How filled with love it is. Her memories feel like a gift and a kick in the gut, all in one.

I guess it isn't surprising. We're made of flesh and bones that wear and tear and sometimes we actually get worn out, just like my hip has decided to do. Somehow, though, I just never believed it would happen to the people I love, to my people. In my mind they would always be as I knew them to be as their younger selves, never-changing. As I hold my mother's hand, déjà vu washes over me. I suppose I shouldn't be surprised. Time takes its toll on all things. Sometimes that toll is gentle, and sometimes it's harsh. As a biologist, I know this is the essence of things. The Second Law of Thermodynamics, the Law of Increased Entropy in action I suppose you could say. It's just much easier reading about it than it is living it.

I've learned a lot about myself in these dementia-colored years. I've had to learn a new way of being. A new way of accepting it is what it is. I've been late to that party, bumping into frustration with how I wish things were, being frustrated with my own lack of understanding, my own lack of patience. My own knee-jerk reaction to thinking No, rather than Yes. Recently I listened to a talk given by two people sharing how Alzheimer's Disease had impacted someone they loved and what they had learned in their care-giving. They shared their observation that we tell people with dementia No all the time. No, it's not 1950. No, you don't live in Spain, saying no to all they're experiencing because of course, reality is the one we're experiencing. We do this in our desire to keep our loved ones as we thought they were, and we end up solidly on the side of No even though our loved ones' minds have been co-opted by this erosive disease. No amount of us saying No is going to change that or make it better. The speakers encouraged "be with the reality before you, and rather than 'No, but' try 'Yes, and.'" Their words spoke to my heart and encouraged me to try a better way.

Yes, and. What a profound shift that would make in all of our relationships. With our kids, partners, parents, friends, dogs, horses. No, but, puts a wall between us. Yes, and, opens doors. Just because they're not the doors we expected, doesn't mean there isn't something for us on the other side. Another lesson for me, in life, and in horses. As always, horsemanship has become a mirror, a metaphor for life to me, running together showing me who I am, who I can be, who I want to be.

Chapter Seventy
What a Long Strange Trip It's Been

All that is gold does not glitter.
Not all those who wander are lost.
The old that is strong does not wither.
Deep roots are not reached by the frost.
J.R.R. Tolkien

I'm the great under-estimator. Or maybe, over-estimator. If someone says something will take an hour, I think it can happen in half that. Sometimes that optimism works well, and other times, well, it's the amuse bouche to another much-needed lesson in patience. I'm still a C+ student with that, so my lessons keep coming. The surgery to give me a new bionic hip was elective, but

I really wasn't keen on the whole let's replace your bones aspect of it. Once the X-Ray had confirmed my hip was shot, it was a flurry of appointments and scheduling. The day was set for the end of September and the great wait began. There's a special dread about waiting for something that has a general sense of yuk about it. I immersed myself in supporting my Mom on her own recovery. My strong farmer Dad was by her side and our family muddled along in what one day we'll fondly recall as the Summer of Fudged Up Hips. When the day of my surgery finally came, I was grateful to be the first surgery out of the gate, with a 5:45 a.m. check-in. There was no turning back and it was time to put away my dread of all things involving saws and hammers, put on my game face and do the damn thing. Last I remember was leaning into a pillow so the anesthesiologist could perform the spinal, and next thing I knew I was in recovery with Pat holding my hand. Just like he had eleven years ago, one of life's strange symmetries. We've spent half our lives together, and just celebrated our twenty-ninth anniversary, aka 203 dog years. Those vows we speak so earnestly yet naively when we begin a marriage have proven themselves to be true portents of the storms we all weather; we just really don't know how true they will prove to be. For better or worse, through sickness and health, to love and cherish. Through all the crazy roads life leads us down, I was grateful to have his hand to hold on to once again.

    It felt good to be on the other side of things; past the waiting and the sense of impending dread, and now on the recovery side. Recovery is its own challenge, but at least you're heading in the right direction. The surgeon had to do a bunch of fiddling around in there to get my hip figured out, so my leg was understandably bent out of shape about it. It was showing its complaints by feeling like a wooden post and not behaving very cooperatively. But later that night, the very nice nurse Ron had me up and cruising the halls, measuring my accomplishment by references to football field distances. You have to welcome your new parts, otherwise they feel unwelcome. I learned this before when my titanium hardware would get a twinge and I'd feel like I'd chewed on a ball of foil. This time, I remembered to say hello to my new bionic hip as we began again. Taking the first steps of a new yet familiar journey. Step by step. One step at a time. The first steps on a new journey of 10,000 steps. I reminded myself, I can do this. I'm no stranger to being taken apart and being put back together.

One morning a wise friend texted me to ask how I was doing, and when I told her things were much different than I'd hoped, she said that maybe I should read a great book by a friend of hers called *Broken, Tales of a Titanium Cowgirl.* And she said, "That girl really figured out how to be with the process."

Snap.

Now that's how you deliver a fine tune-up with a smile.

I have the best friends.

Chapter Seventy-One

The Tortoise and the Hare

Life. Make it work.
Anonymous

Sundance took his usual detour this morning as I was moving horses from here to there, my morning routine, and his too it seems. He eats separately from the rest of the crew, one of the blessings and curses of being the oldest guy here. I don't halter him when it's time to turn him out to join the others. I could, and maybe I should, but he enjoys his detour into the barn to pick at the hay he can't chew (it makes him feel young) and to try to sneak into the barrels of his special old man food. He's incredibly talented at opening the lids with his precocious lips. It's kind of annoying and kind of endearing, and that's how we do it around here. Maybe not always choosing the easiest way, but always the most entertaining. I'm moving slowly but better than I was and I'm grateful for each small step forward. Just being back near the horses helps me feel like I'm back on the road to being me again, but with an extra-dose of bionic.

The weather has personality disorder syndrome. Spring felt like summer, summer felt like summer on steroids, and fall isn't sure what's going on. It was 80 degrees yesterday, 85 today, and predicted to drop to 64 degrees tomorrow. The flies don't miss any opportunity to be bothersome and the warm weather brings them coming from who knows where and pestering the horses. I finished my chores and went to shoosh Sundance back to where he's supposed to go. As I was putting a fly mask on Sundance, trying to get his old ears into the ear spots I thought wow, some of these horses are getting OLD. My grandparents were right about time picking up speed as we become older. Looks like it happens to horses, too. When I began my horsemanship journey my boys were young, now they're amazing young men. Some of my friends are becoming grandparents; some of us are experiencing that slow-drip pain of watching our parents' health fail; some of us are battling our own challenging health issues, saying goodbye to too many people we love.

Taylor Swift and horses have something right; sometimes you've just gotta shake it off. I shook my head, shook out my arms, and took a deep breath; a sure-fire reset. When things are too big for my brain to process, my breath is a reliable compass pointing me back to true north. Back into this moment, not looking back or leaping forward. Sundance ambles off to join his friends, in the moment of course, enjoying the sunshine warming his old bony body. True looks up from scrounging for crumbs and they give each other a peaceful glance, and go back to what they're doing. Horse stuff. There were days I thought this would never happen. That the five of them would never be a peaceful herd but go figure, time is the great washing machine.

Sometimes we look across our lives and wonder what we could have, should have, might have, and never did, differently. I learned about coulda, shoulda, wouldas early in life and I hate them. Regret is the biggest joy killer around. It reminds me of the quote Harry Whitney loves to say, "good judgment comes from experience, and experience comes from bad judgment." There's nothing like experience to give you the opportunity to reshape your perspective.

Maybe how we decide to approach life, and horsemanship, comes down to whether we take on a short-game or a long-game perspective. It's not easy to get away from that instant gratification perspective. We're bombarded with it. Fast food, fast fashion, fast emotions from social media. In 2000, our collective attention span was 12 seconds, now it's right around eight. For perspective, a goldfish's is nine seconds. Nicely played goldfish, nicely played. Information floods at us all the time, but how much of it is worthy of our attention? How much of it is real, how much of it has heart at the heart of it, and how much of it is designed to trip our dopamine fix? The short game is in our faces all the time but that's why I love horses and this journey so much. Horses are free of the clock; and when we step into relationship with them, we have the opportunity to be clock-free, too. That's what the tortoise and the hare were trying to teach us, I guess. I started off on Team Rabbit, and ended up on Team Tortoise. Slow and steady wins the race. If we're lucky, life's a marathon, not a sprint. I've accepted that I've chosen the long game. One step at a time out of a journey of 10,000 steps. It all begins the same way; the decision to make the first step. Then the next, and the next. That steps you one step closer to harmony. One step closer to joy. One step closer to feeling like you're living with your finger on the pulse of the beautiful world animals graciously allow us to experience.

True didn't mind his time off. He spent it wisely by proving he is an extremely easy-keeper. I think he could gain weight off of air. He's put on some pounds that will serve him well this winter. And though I'm not sure when I will be throwing this newly enhanced leg over his back again, I look forward to re-introducing myself to him just like when we began. Small steps, spending time together, listening to him, and learning from him. And I know that by spring, or possibly some beautiful sunny day this winter, I'll throw my leg over the saddle once again. Only this time it will be True saying, "Ride me," and I will remember how it felt all those years ago in the spirit of the great horse who went before him, Simba.

I've been blessed by the teachers along this journey.

Human and horses.

The horses head off to the high pasture and I hobble back to the four-wheeler, reminding myself to walk like a boss and not like I'm broken. I remind myself, this isn't my first rodeo, and it takes the time it takes. My new bionic parts will take me forward step by step just like my titanium parts did all those years ago. This morning when I closed my eyes and stood in the sunshine, sending up prayers of gratitude, I heard very clearly, be still and know that I am God.

Got it.

I hope wherever you are, whatever is going on in your life, that you are finding peace in being with what is on this new never to be experienced again day.

Whatever that is for you.

Our horses are already so good at it.

These lessons are good for my human-ship and my horsemanship.

Chapter Seventy-Two

Grace

I do not understand the mystery of grace—only that it meets us where we are and does not leave us where it found us.
Anne Lamott

We all come to horsemanship (and life) through a variety of experiences. Sometimes a wreck or a scare drove us to look for help. Other times it's a feeling that there's something missing in a relationship between our horses and ourselves that has us looking for a different way. Grace is a powerful starting place. Grace isn't something we often talk about with horses, but I'm pretty sure we could all benefit from a good dose of grace for ourselves, and for our horses.

Be gracious with yourself; if we're doing this horsemanship journey, we always will be students and there always will be more to learn. Learning requires opening yourself up to uncertainty and vulnerability. That's okay. It's better than okay; it's a beautiful thing, really. In horsemanship (and life) the more you look, the more you learn. And go figure, the more you learn, the more you realize you don't know, and the more you want to learn. That's how it becomes a journey rather than a path. There's no gadget that will get you there, only you, your heart, and your horse. Sometimes it feels more like one step forward, ten steps back. But keep stepping. Even in those times where it feels like we're stuck, we can still be thankful to our horses for the lessons. Mine are teaching me way more than I will ever teach them. True would swear to it.

Be gracious with your horse. Unfortunately, some of the crazy stuff humans cook up to do with, and to, horses can really put worry into their lives and it can show up in little ways or big ways. Some of the crazy stuff we do to ourselves can make our own worry bubble over too. Like Charley Snell reminds us, horses are looking for peace. It's our job and privilege to help them find it. With us. When peace feels hard to find, smile. Don't ask me how, but it works.

Being on a journey means there's always new country to see, new lessons to learn. Pat yourself and your horse on the back for looking for better ways to be together. The horse world has some very dark spots; be gracious with yourself for standing in the light.

Grace. Saying it softly to myself before I even touch my horse feels like a benediction over the things we will do together. With grace in place, it's hard to go too far wrong. In fact, it might just be impossible.

> *Almost everything will work if you unplug it for a few seconds, including you.*
> Anne Lamott

Chapter Seventy-Three

Thank You

*Life is a marathon, not a sprint.
Pace yourself accordingly.
Amby Burfoot*

It's okay y'all.
Okay to be struggling, okay to question, okay to think "if only."
Believe me when I say that all things can be used for your good, in ways you could never imagine.

Faith, family, and friends can see you through.
And I am so grateful for all of you.
Thank you for joining me on this journey of horsemanship and life.
I was just telling someone that all the people I truly treasure have a tendency to be incredibly authentic and that's fine with me.
Being real and all of its permutations is not something to be ashamed of, or to shy away from, but to be embraced.
It may be messy, but hey, we're all works in progress.
And that's a good thing.
Every day is a new chance to begin again.
Life. It's not often what we were expecting it would be but my heart is raw and wide open to the miracle of second chances.

If you woke up this morning, today's a second chance y'all.
Let's go out there and be freaking AWESOME.

Let us run with endurance the race set before us.
Hebrews 12.1

The End

(Kind of...)

Appendix
Horsemanship and Life: Asking from a Friend

I don't know where I'm going from here, but I promise it won't be boring.
David Bowie

Mark Rashid once said, and it's stuck with me, is that life's an opportunity to practice horsemanship. Mark wasn't kidding; standing in the twenty-person deep line in the grocery store gives me all the practice I can handle. One day I got a wild hair to ask some of my favorite horse people, "Hey, when I say 'Horsemanship and Life' to you, what comes to mind, and would you share a few words, paragraphs, thoughts?" And go figure, they were kind enough not to laugh and they took the time to share their thoughts with us. Which just proved I was right in picking them in the first place. I'm grateful to know that there are people out there who are all about the horse, and that they're leading with heart and integrity. I'm grateful to every one of them who are out there shining a light for all of us who are looking for a better way for our horses.

Like Buck Brannaman said, "Horses and life, it's all the same to me."

And just like that, all roads lead back to that rabbit. And horses, of course.

Definition: get a wild hair
A wild hair is a phenomenon found around horses. A hair from the horse's tail may fall into the water trough. Sometimes fungus or mold on the hair will make the hair wriggle through the water as if it were alive.

Crissi McDonald, Heartline Horse Training

I met Crissi years ago at a clinic, at the same time I met Mark Rashid. Crissi's gentle kindness settled my nerves immediately, but it didn't take long to realize that underneath that calm exterior was a razor-sharp sense of humor. I was sold. Crissi talked me off the ledge a time or two when I was going stir-crazy after my wreck, and it's been a joy to watch her horsemanship and life journey in all the years since. Beyond offering lessons and teaching clinics with her husband Mark Rashid, Crissi's a Masterson Method® equine body worker and an instructor for the Masterson two-day Beyond Horse Massage workshops. Crissi's the author of two horsemanship books, and has now expanded her talents to fiction and will soon be releasing her second fiction book.

Crissi's words:

It's a truth that how we do one thing is how we do everything. Horses, and learning how to get along with them, offer a unique opportunity for us to explore this truth. They are tolerant enough to seek to work with us. They are unselfconscious in their beauty and athleticism. They make zero apologies for who they are. And we can rely on who they are: they don't deceive us or themselves. Maybe this is one of the many reasons those of us whose lives revolve around horses are so passionate about learning how to find closer relationships with them. They are living examples of authenticity and connection.

Humans can be a species of absolutes and boxes. As humans, we filter and relate to our world through labels, political parties, our senses, and the mosaic of the beliefs we've cultivated based on our life experiences. This isn't necessarily bad: the way our brains have evolved and the current culture we find ourselves in makes it a challenge to go through life any other way.

But if we choose to involve ourselves with horses, those boxes and labels and stories (both true and not true) will get thrown out of the saddle and left in the dust. Horses, like most things in nature, are creatures of purity. What they are is a product of an evolutionary path that is fifty million years older than our own. They live by senses we seek to ignore or haven't even learned we can utilize. If we listen closely, however, we can learn to access those same senses, too. We can work on that one thing we find important, whether we're with our horses or not.

Much of my life has been spent exploring ways to cross-pollinate what I do with horses into what I do within my life. Middle age has found me with a few more dents and dings. Maybe by now I've had some sense knocked into me. These days my "one thing" practice is listening. If I can listen with my body as well as my ears, if I can listen through my guts as well as through my eyes, being with horses is an exciting journey of discovery. When I'm not with horses, listening to the person or people around me, as well as nature, helps me hone and broaden this skill. Whether it is my life with horses, or my life doing other things, how I do this one activity will help me with everything else.

I don't think life and horsemanship are that far apart. I think there's life and the things we choose to fill the time we are given. Horses are an elegant and arresting way to spend our days, especially knowing that we can use our time with them to find the one thing that is most important to us.

Josh Nichol, Relational Horsemanship

Josh Nichol learned from some of the greatest horsemen of our time, who noticed his gift with horses and mentored him. Josh is one of those people you can't help but be struck by. Not only is he an extraordinary horseman, but he has what I've come to call relentless positivity. Josh's approach, Relational Horsemanship, is built on a foundation of forming a deep connection with horses by seeking to understand their needs to help empower rather than dominate. His approach integrates the desire we have to build a true relationship with our horses and inspires us to understand what motivates our own needs and inner life so that we can show up as our best selves to our horses. I don't remember when I first learned of Josh, but in the years since I've admired and followed his horsemanship, I've had my eyes opened in so many ways to what can be. In my horses, and in me.

Josh's words:

Discovering Your Deeper Self Through Horsemanship...when it comes to learning, I have always been a deep-diver. I prefer to take a bit more time in order to think about the details and complexities of a subject because I truly want to understand at a deep level. This desire to go deep has benefited me time and time again in my pursuit of horsemanship. My thirst for learning has taken me all over the place, from colt-starting at ranches to riding with seasoned horsemen and classical dressage masters. One of the greatest gifts of working with a wide variety of horses in a number of different disciplines is that I have been continually confronted with the common denominator in each interaction: myself. So while I certainly care about good techniques and proper equipment, I think that the most important thing in great horsemanship is self-awareness and the ability to show up for our horses in a way that they genuinely desire to be with. When we can do that, the lessons we learn don't just help us in the riding arena; the insights we receive from our horses have the potential to change our entire lives. Here are just a few of the insights from horses that have been especially important to me.

If we desire to build great relationships with horses (and people), communicating well is crucial. When two beings engage in conversation, it is important to understand that each party brings their own "stuff" to the interaction—the experiences, beliefs, and lenses through which they see the world that uniquely shape the energy they bring to the space. I have noticed one of the biggest breakdowns in communication is reacting poorly and feeling justified in our negative reactions because of what has been said or done to us first. For example, if a person makes a negative comment to us, we might feel justified to yell at them. Or if a horse kicks out, we interpret that as a personal attack and lash out at the horse in anger. It can be easy to feel justified in these reactions and use our pressure emotionally because we are focusing solely on what has been done to us.

Unfortunately, we often use far more pressure than we need to and we miss that gut feeling that tells us to stop because we are locked onto the unjust actions of the other (based on our interpretations) and we get emotionally swept up in our reactions. The challenge is that our interpretation does not consider how we personally are showing up in the space and then we get "baited" into reacting to the other, which actually means that they are leading the interaction.

I have found that when interactions go sideways, it can usually be traced back to (a) the choices I have made and (b) the energy I have put into the interaction (which at the time may have felt very justified). However, when I suspend my judgments and interpretations of the other's behavior and replace it with curiosity, the conversation becomes far more productive. In addition, we can shift our focus from what others are doing and choose to be more mindful of what we are bringing to the interaction. This concept is not limited to horses or people but rather is a way of looking at life. I would say that this shift in perspective has had the biggest impact on my life and my growth as a human and brings me to one of my favorite quotes by Socrates: "know thyself."

This little phrase has been so powerful for me because it turns my curiosity inward to the part I play in my relationships. I hope that it can inspire a similar shift in you so that you realize you have a great deal of power when it comes to the way you show up in the world. At any moment, you can learn more about yourself by noticing your thoughts, feelings and actions in relation to what is happening around you. The beginning of change happens when we first pause, take a step back, and reflect on the way we think. You are not responsible for anyone else's behavior but you do have a lot of control over your own actions. Our behavior often begins with our thoughts and the way we interpret interactions. Your interpretation has the power to move energy in entirely new ways and can either tear relationships down or build them up; the choice is yours.

The key is to become responsible for your own thoughts and actions and release everything else. When we let go of the need to control others, we can start to look within and start our own pursuits of self-awareness. Over the years, there have been many moments, especially with the horses, that have challenged the way I look at life. Horses are always giving us feedback about the patterns and tendencies they feel from us as we show up in relationships. One of the main goals I have for my students (and myself) is to receive the feedback the horses offer us with grace and curiosity. It reminds me of another quote from Carl Rogers:

"We think we listen, but very rarely do we listen with real under-

standing, true empathy. Yet listening, of this very special kind, is one of the most potent forces for change that I know."
- Carl Rogers

I believe that listening is a super power. When we listen from a place of self-awareness and being grounded in the present moment, we have a much better chance of truly hearing what the horse or person in front of us is saying. Sometimes it can be difficult to know if we are truly hearing the other, especially when it comes to horses, so I pay close attention to what brings the horse peace. A congruent expression of peace has been the best indicator that I have found to tell me that I have understood and gotten to the heart of what matters to the horse (or person). When our thinking comes from a place of inner peace and we can listen to understand rather than listen to speak, we begin to truly hear the needs of others.

Once we have developed the ability to hear the needs of others, we can respond in a way that brings more peace to those around us. By taking responsibility for yourself, you can continually shift your focus away from what others are doing and put more energy into being the change you want to see in the world. My hope is that we can all feel more liberated from the relational patterns that perpetuate dysfunction and instead lean into the peace and connection that the horses naturally embody. The last thought I'll leave you with is this: when something in life does not go as planned, pay attention to what comes up for you. When we are caught off guard, we often get a more honest look at what is happening for us underneath the surface. Instead of seeing these moments exclusively as problems, there is so much potential to gain valuable insights about your thinking patterns and use the challenge as an opportunity to adapt and grow.

Mark Rashid, Considering the Horse

I met Mark Rashid at a clinic years ago. Though he's an internationally-known horseman and prolific author, his amiable demeanor, easy-going personality immediately dispelled whatever nerves I had. Mark is a remarkable horseman, but also an onion. As the years go by, I'm more amazed all the time at the layers of creativity in one man. He studied Yoshinkan aikido to enhance his horsemanship, and became a second-degree black belt and now teaches "the way of harmony" as well as Aikido for Horseman workshops. If that didn't keep him busy enough, he's written over a dozen horsemanship books, a fiction novel *Out of the Wild* which was made into a (good) movie, plays guitars, makes guitars, and is a musician with his friend Brad Fitch. All in his spare time. I'll never forget Mark telling me that life was an opportunity to practice horsemanship, so I couldn't wait to ask him if he would answer my question: Horsemanship-and-Life.

Mark's words:

When I think about how closely horsemanship and life are connected, my mind is immediately drawn to a concept I was first introduced to many years ago during the early days of my training in the martial art of aikido. In Japanese the term is Mizu no Kokoro. Translated, it means "a mind (or heart) like water." In some circles it is translated to mean "a mind like still water."

The goal in developing *Mizu no Kokoro* is to train the mind to become quiet and still, like a lake or pond in the early morning when there is no wind, and where the surface of the water becomes mirror-like. Developing this stillness in ourselves allows us to see things we encounter in life in mirror image, as they really are, without embellishment or judgment. *Mizu no Kokoro* encourages us to give up our internal dialog and the need to make up stories (sometimes accurate, sometimes not) around our daily encounters so we can lead a more peaceful and productive existence.

It's important to understand that *Mizu no Kokoro* isn't necessarily about being perpetually calm, but rather the idea encourages us to develop a mind like water—flowing, reflective, and adaptive.

A pebble tossed into a mirror-like pond will disrupt the stillness of the water. Ripples travel outward from the point of impact, eventually affecting every inch of the pond's surface. The water itself doesn't try to stop the disturbance, nor does the water add to it. It simply allows the disturbance to take its course until it exhausts itself. As those ripples complete their outward-bound journey all the way to the edge of the pond's banks, they then disappear into the shoreline. The water once again smoothes out and returns to its original quiet, mirror-like state.

The practice of *Mizu no Kokoro* allows us that same ability—to return to a quiet state of mind in a relatively short period of time (as opposed to days, weeks, months, or even years) when the events and stresses of our lives create internal disturbances. Things that unsettle us in our life, or in our horsemanship, are like that pebble in the pond, and ripples are inevitable. It's the way we handle those ripples that dictates how much they affect us, our life, and our work with horses.

Molly Sanders, Shine a Light Productions

I was excited to ask Molly for her thoughts when I threw out "horsemanship and life" as I've watched her expand both the past two years. Molly and I met when she hosted a virtual clinic with Charley Snell during the height of the pandemic. I was impressed with anyone who managed to get a Montana cowboy to do a virtual anything. We both love learning from Charley and we became immediate friends. Molly began her horsemanship journey as a high-level Parelli instructor and is in an evolution in her pursuit of horsemanship. Whereas I perfected the perfect spicy margarita during the pandemic, Molly used the huge shift to begin her own podcast and Facebook group, A Learner's Journey.

Molly's words:

Intertwined, inseparable are two words that came to mind when Michelle first invited me to share about Horsemanship and Life. I'm sure you can relate when I say that I connect everything back to horses—everything!

Lessons I've learned from horses have guided me through some pretty challenging times.

I'd like to share two examples of horsemanship lessons I've learned that have helped me in other areas. One is a lesson I learned over a decade ago and the other, I'm in the middle of learning now.

Lesson from the past: "How interesting!" This phrase was shared with me almost 20 years ago when I first started exploring horsemanship through the Parelli program. It's a phrase Linda Parelli shared on a DVD I was studying. She was coaching students to shift their mindset when they were getting frustrated with their horse's behavior. Instead of saying, "no!" or "stop it" or one of the other phrases I wouldn't type in a family-friendly book... replace it with "how interesting." "How interesting," shifts the way we look at it. We can trigger our brains to move toward curiosity and problem solving instead of staying in an ego-centric thought pattern; "why are you doing this to me?" This made a dramatic shift in my horsemanship at that time and since has helped me in other areas of life.

I recently had a challenge in my virtual course-creation business, Shine a Light Productions. A course I thought was going to be a grand slam—one that the community would love—started off with crickets as a response.... I first went into the ego-centric mode, "why me?" "Is it something I did?" Then after a morning spent with those thoughts, I sat back and thought, "how interesting"... Solution-seeking shift complete.

If you haven't tried this phrase out yet, I'd highly recommend it. Our brains like searching for solutions. Put them to work finding one.

Lesson currently in the works: This lesson is one I'm in the middle of learning. It comes from my time spent with a very special horseman named Charley Snell. He often says that "good movement produces a good feeling and ill movement produces ill feelings."

Good movement = moving forward in a gait with a relaxed, attentive, and responsive mind. Also, stepping under with the hindquarter while staying free in the front (not planting the front end down) can relax a horse and encourage them to let go of a worried thought.

I had a light bulb moment the other day when I was walking along—heavy on the front end, shoulders slouched, and feeling a bit discouraged with the state of affairs.... I was moving poorly and was producing similar feelings! I changed my posture and my stride and voila, my feelings changed instantly.

Horsemanship is a way to view the world. It becomes a part of us, a guide for living a quality life. I'm forever grateful for the lessons horses share, I'm by far a better person because of them.

Shea Stewart, Equine Balance

I asked Shea to share her thoughts on horsemanship-life as I've long admired how encompassing her work with horses is. Her approach is uniquely holistic. She has extensive experience in equine clinical practice, body work, and craniosacral. Her approach to horsemanship is focused on relationship and holistic health and bodywork. Her years of instruction in anatomy, behavior, biomechanics, nutrition, and body work to support horses have led her on a journey to help people connect in a meaningful way with their horses. Her journey continues to expand, from helping horses function optimally in body and mind. She's committed to helping people with their horses through lessons, consultations, but most especially in support-

ing their desire to connect with their horses on a deeper level.
Shea's words:

My goal in my horsemanship journey was to connect to the heart and mind of the horse, and to help people have a better understanding of the possibilities of this connection. What I started to learn along the way was how this relationship with horses can be incredibly healing for the human. Communicating with a horse by exchanging a heartfelt feel brings us into an awareness of our own self-concept, our own embodiment, our own rhythms in how we walk through life. This relationship with horses taught me how to slow down my mind and pay attention, have faith in the present moment.

Horses are incredibly grounding and thrive on a meaningful connection. Their expressive energy can bring awareness to aspects of ourselves that lay deep inside. And always there to remind us when our mind loses connection to the present moment. Every horse that I worked
with gave me an opportunity to become more aware, and aligned to my true nature. As my system began to settle and regulate to the slower rhythms in which a horse lives, my life began to transform to a more meaningful, rich, and colorful world. Bringing awareness of the interconnectedness of all life and the peace this brings through its simplicity. Every horse who came in with trauma, gave me the gift of healing myself. I learned that emotional triggers were pieces that haven't yet been healed, and to have patience when I didn't have the answers. As the answers can be found in stillness.

Tom Moates, Spinning Sevens Press, Horseman/Author

Tom is an award-winning equestrian writer and author; his hundreds of articles have been in all the notable equine publications. Tom came to horsemanship in a circuitous way, as do many of us, and coming upon Harry Whitney was a game-changer for him. Harry and Tom have been close friends for years and he's the guy who captured the elusive Mr. Whitney's thoughts into books such as *Between the Reins*, to his latest, the last of the triad *Six Colts, Two Weeks*. Tom published TWO new books this year, including a compilation of essays, *Mane Thoughts*. I have no idea how he gets so much done in between writing, publishing, teaching, learning, and taking care of his herd of horses. He's also my very kind, very encouraging publisher and my book exists because he believed in it and me.

Tom's words:

Horsemanship is a malleable mindset, made magnificent most masterfully by the mild-mannered man (or woman, naturally) meaning to re-move mistrust and "misbehavior" in a matchless manner by messaging real meaning to the horse by means of matching mind to mind and movement to movement.

Life is a gift from God, generating glory because of His generosity.

I considered just leaving my reply to Michelle's inquiry for a couple of paragraphs on my thoughts on horsemanship and life at that. But then, I wasn't sure that Michelle's intentions really were addressed there, although that does kinda sum things up, and with some serious alliteration!

As to horsemanship and life, to expound a bit....

Both horsemanship and life share the central hinge point of relationship. They both are about developing relationships and gaining the skills to open ourselves up to being capable of better relationships. And central to both are thinking—that is, that our minds are the means to maturing in both horsemanship and life, and yet there is a significant measure of feel involved, as well, that also must be acknowledged.

Horsemanship, in my mind, is the skill of setting up the relationship between the horse and the human. If the relationship is right, then we have a horse who thinks along with our requests. Rather than a mechanical endeavor, like pulling on a rein, the relationship can be based on a true communication where a slight feel put on a rein with a finger is all it takes to have a horse think in a direction and go there willingly.

Life is, well, a gift from God wherein we have the chance to make choices and constantly enjoy (or, at least, engage) the challenges we come up against. Hopefully we grow, and that our relationship with God thereby grows. And therein, as God commands, love Him with all of our heart, soul, and mind, and to love thy neighbor as thyself, we ought to likewise see relationships with others also develop. And this also ought not to be a mechanical endeavor (works), but rather that we learn to recognize God's feel present on the reins of our lives and have increasing faith in Him that can produce willingness to follow in us.

So that kinda kicks it around some more in two...oh no, wait, more like seven paragraphs! Woops...sorry Michelle; I never could follow directions!

About the Author

Michelle R. Scully earned her B. S. in Zoology (go Aggies!) and M.S. in Biology, which makes her a science geek and perpetual student of nature and animals. She's most grateful to have kept a child's sense of wonder as it keeps her in awe and never bored. In between caring for a crew of horses, some more than happily retired, she tries to keep up with her wild dog duo and takes instruction from one cat. She describes her aesthetic as cowgirl, bohemian, lumber jack, and old man. She and her husband Pat are blessed with two amazing adult sons who also indulge her fervent love of animals. They live in northern California and are proud to be part of the 1% in farming. This is her second book.

www.ingramcontent.com/pod-product-compliance
Lightning Source LLC
Chambersburg PA
CBHW020353170426
43200CB00005B/156